QUOD SEMP... ...IQUE

QUOD AB OMNIBUS

NORTH CAROLINA DURING RECONSTRUCTION

RICHARD L. ZUBER

RALEIGH
DIVISION OF ARCHIVES AND HISTORY
NORTH CAROLINA DEPARTMENT OF CULTURAL RESOURCES

CONTENTS

ILLUSTRATIONS

FOREWORD

In 1969 the Department (now Division) of Archives and History filled a void in North Carolina historiography by publishing a brief history titled *North Carolina during Reconstruction*. The booklet was written by Richard L. Zuber, then an associate professor at Wake Forest University and author of the book *Jonathan Worth: A Biography of a Southern Unionist*. In 1975 *North Carolina during Reconstruction* underwent a second printing and then sold out again in 1987. Because of budgetary restraints, the title—which sold nearly 10,000 copies in its first two printings—has remained out of print for almost a decade. Now the Historical Publications Section is again pleased to offer this important work to the public. Written by a respected authority on the Reconstruction era, it provides a fascinating summary of political, social, and economic events in the Tar Heel State during the tumultuous period following the Civil War.

Joe A. Mobley, *Administrator*
Historical Publications Section

July 1996

William W. Holden, a key figure in North Carolina during the Reconstruction period, was the only North Carolina governor ever impeached. Photograph from the North Carolina Collection, University of North Carolina at Chapel Hill.

NORTH CAROLINA DURING RECONSTRUCTION

The armies of General Joseph E. Johnston and General William T. Sherman fought the last major battle of the Civil War at Bentonville, North Carolina, near the end of March, 1865. Three weeks later Sherman's men marched into the state capital at Raleigh. On April 26 General Johnston, realizing that further military resistance to the Union was useless, surrendered his army to General Sherman. Governor Zebulon B. Vance had fled to Statesville in advance of the occupation of Raleigh; it was in Statesville that he was arrested on May 14 and taken to a prison in Washington, D.C., for several weeks. For North Carolina, and for the nation, the Civil War was over.

The war had damaged North Carolina in several ways. Most tragic of all the effects of the conflict was the death of over 40,000 of the state's best men. Both state and local governments had collapsed at the end of the war. One of the main sources of labor had seemed to disappear when the slaves gained their freedom. The banks, which would be needed to help restore the

Negotiations between Generals Sherman and Johnston took place at the house of James Bennett on April 18, 1865. The Bennett Place, located near Durham, is now open to the public as one of the state's historic sites. This drawing is from Frank Leslie's illustrations in *The American Soldier in the Civil War.*

state's economic system, were about to fail because they had lent money to the Confederacy and to the state and would never be repaid. The colleges, the university, and the public schools had all suffered as a result of wartime conditions. Now it was doubtful whether those that had closed could reopen and whether those that were still open could continue to operate. Countless individuals had borne losses of both loved ones and possessions that could never be replaced.

In spite of the general bleakness of conditions in the state, there was some hope. North Carolina had always been basically a land of farmers, and the land remained. The armies had done much damage, to be sure, but most of the state had seen little destruction and few men on the march. The abundant natural resources of minerals and forests were still waiting for the miner, the lumberman, and the furniture maker. Some men could see these signs of hope, and even those who felt gloomy about the future were willing to work hard to regain what they had lost.

GENERAL SCHOFIELD

North Carolina was under military rule throughout the year 1865. When General Sherman left the state in April he placed

General John M. Schofield in charge. Schofield's main job was to maintain law and order, but he also was concerned with the welfare of the freed Negroes. He issued a statement that the war was over and that slavery no longer existed. Then he arranged for each county to have a police force and tried to find local officials who had favored the Union in the war.

General John Schofield was put in charge of North Carolina when General Sherman left the state in April, 1865. This photograph and others, except where otherwise specified, are from the files of the State Department of Archives and History.

THE PRESIDENT'S RECONSTRUCTION PLAN

With the Union army still in control of the South, President Andrew Johnson had to decide what to do with North Carolina and the other southern states. He announced his policies in two proclamations issued on May 29, 1865. The first of these proclamations applied to the whole South. It pardoned those who had rebelled against the national government, except the most out-

2

standing leaders and the men of considerable wealth; it specified an oath to be taken by those who wanted to be pardoned; and it said southerners could keep all their property except their former slaves.

President Andrew Johnson, a native North Carolinian, appointed William W. Holden provisional governor of the state.

Johnson's second proclamation, the first of a series of similar proclamations for the states of the South, applied only to North Carolina. In it he appointed William W. Holden to serve as provisional governor until a normal state government could be restored. Holden was one of the most interesting and important men of the Civil War and Reconstruction periods. Before the war he had been a strong spokesman for southern rights, but during the war he was a stern critic of Jefferson Davis and the Confederacy. It was probably because of the way he had acted during the war that the President appointed him provisional governor.

After announcing Holden's appointment, the North Carolina proclamation stated that he would call a convention to reorganize the state government and get North Carolina back into the union. Anyone who had been a voter before the war and had been pardoned for his part in the war could vote for delegates to the convention. The proclamation directed the military authorities in the state to help Holden with his work.

Governor Holden soon issued a statement explaining further how the government was to be restored and how the state could once again become a member of the federal union. The 1865 convention was supposed to repeal the 1861 ordinance that took North Carolina out of the union, officially abolish slavery, and cancel the state's debt for war expenses. The convention would also provide for the election of a governor, a state legislature, and members of the national House of Representatives. The legislature itself would select two United States senators. When the state officers were sworn in, civilian government would be restored. If Congress would admit the representatives and senators at its next session, North Carolina would be back in the union.

CONVENTION OF 1865

The convention met in October, 1865. Its first actions were the repeal of the ordinance of secession and the abolition of slavery. The question of what to do about the state debt caused the most trouble. If the debt were repudiated, or canceled, many individuals would lose their fortunes, the banks would be bankrupt, and both the university and the public school system would be damaged. During the convention Governor Holden demanded that the debt be repudiated and got a letter from President Johnson backing up his demand. Most historians think he did this because he wanted to become the regular governor at the next election.

ELECTION OF 1865

The convention arranged for a state election to be held in November; members of Congress, a governor, legislators, and some local officers were to be chosen. While the convention was still in session, Jonathan Worth, the treasurer in the provisional government, announced that he was running for governor against Holden. Worth had always been a strong union man, although he had served as state treasurer during the war. During the campaign Holden's followers tried to get the people to believe that if Worth were elected North Carolina would not be allowed to come back into the union. But Worth was elected anyway. Many people apparently were angry with Holden because he had forced the convention to repudiate the war debt. Others distrusted Holden because he had often changed his position on important issues in the past and it was hard to tell exactly what he stood for.

The men chosen to represent North Carolina in the national House of Representatives were friends of the Union, but when they reported to Washington they were not allowed to take their seats. The United States senators chosen by the new legislature, William A. Graham and John Pool, also were former Whigs and Unionists, but they were not allowed to become members of

4

Governor Jonathan Worth, treasurer in the provisional government, ran for governor against Holden and was elected in 1865.

the Senate. The refusal by Congress to admit the representatives and senators from North Carolina meant that the state would not be back in the national government officially until two and a half years later.

THE RADICALS

When Congress refused to seat the delegates from North Carolina, and other southern states, it became obvious that the fate of the states depended largely upon what was happening in Washington. If the President had had his way North Carolina would have been back in the union late in 1865 or early in 1866. But by that time a Republican faction in Congress known as the Radicals was beginning to insist that Congress, rather than the President, should decide when and on what terms the southern states would be allowed to return to the union. Some Radicals felt that the South ought to be changed before it came back. Some were deeply concerned about the newly freed Negroes and wanted to be sure that they would not be returned to a condition like slavery. And some of the Radicals wanted to gives the Negroes the right to vote so they would support the Republicans in the future. Whatever their reasons, the Radicals determined to block President Johnson's plan of reconstruction. That is why they refused to admit southerners to Congress and began to pass laws to protect the Negroes.

By this time the question of what to do about the freed Negroes had become the most difficult and most important problem facing North Carolina. About 350,000 Negroes in the state had been freed by the Thirteenth Amendment, and everyone admitted that slavery was gone forever. But that left a series of puzzling questions. Should the freedmen be allowed to vote? Should they be allowed to serve on juries and to testify in court against white men? Should they ride in the same railroad cars, eat in the same places, and go to the same schools? Late in 1865 Governor Holden appointed a commission of three distinguished lawyers to study the Negro question and recommend to the legislature a set of laws stating and guaranteeing the rights of the freedmen. Early in 1866 the legislature enacted a "Black Code" based on the report of the commission. Most of the provisions of the black code were favorable to the Negroes; their marriages were made legal; they were to be trained for various occupations in the same way as white people; and their rights in making contracts were to be safeguarded. Unfortunately, in spite of efforts to be fair, there was discrimination against the Negroes in the new legal code. A Negro man who assaulted a white woman was to be punished more severely than a white man, and the legislature at this time refused to allow Negroes to testify in court. Neither were they given the right to vote.

Even before North Carolina and the other southern states began passing their black codes the federal government had set up an extensive program to assist both Negroes and whites who had been displaced by the war and were in need of food, clothing, and shelter. This program was carried out by an agency called officially the Bureau of Freedmen, Refugees, and Abandoned Lands, but known usually as the Freedmen's Bureau. It was in operation in North Carolina from July, 1865, down to the end of 1868. Most of the bureau's work was designed to meet the existing needs of the freedmen, but it also began helping them prepare for their future. Over four hundred schools were set up, and soon the Negroes, young and old, were trying to secure the simple education which had been denied to them as slaves. The bureau doled out about two million meals, mostly to Negroes, but sometimes to needy whites. Clothing too was available. About 40,000 people received treatment in bureau hospitals. The bureau also assisted the Negroes by helping them work out labor contracts with their white em-

Peace College, chartered in 1857, was opened in 1872; its main building, shown here, was used as a Confederate hospital and later as the Freedmen's Bureau headquarters.

ployers. Most of the work of the bureau was done by northern soldiers, but many civilians worked with the soldiers. Especially prominent was the work of the "Yankee school ma'ams" who taught the Negro children in the bureau schools.

Many North Carolinians disliked the Freedmen's Bureau and the work it was doing. They thought that the Negroes would not go to work on the farms if the government continued to give them food and clothing. White farmers did not want the bureau agents to butt in when they were trying to work out labor contracts with Negro workers. Governor Worth and some of the judges and lawyers were annoyed because the bureau interfered with the state courts when Negroes were being tried. Sometimes the bureau set up courts of its own and tried Negroes, rather than allowing them to be tried by the regular North Carolina courts. In some cases advice given by the northern whites seemed to make the Negroes more willing to defy the wishes of the men who had formerly been their masters. Finally, and worst of all in the opinion of men who despised the bureau, was the fact that bureau agents and schoolteachers were teaching the Negroes about politics and making them supporters of the Radical plan of reconstruction.

THE FOURTEENTH AMENDMENT

The first Freedmen's Bureau was set up to last only one year. Early in 1866 Congress passed a bill extending the life and the work of the bureau. President Johnson vetoed the bill, but Congress overrode his veto. The same thing happened to the Civil Rights Act of 1866, which the national government attempted to make the Negroes citizens of the states and guarantee that they would receive "equal benefit of all laws." But the thing which Congress did that had the most effect on North Carolina and further divided Congress and the President was to draw up and send to the states for approval the Fourteenth Amendment to the United States Constitution. The amendment stated that Negroes were citizens and that states could not take away their rights. States which denied Negroes the right to vote were to have the number of their representatives in Congress reduced. Under the amendment no one who had sworn to support the Constitution of the United States and then supported the Confederacy would be allowed to hold public office. Congress seemed to be trying to protect the Negroes and to punish the South at the same time. Although there was no law saying so, it was understood that the southern states would have to ratify the Fourteenth Amendment before they could get back into the union. To put it another way, Congress would not admit the representatives and senators from a given state until that state had approved the amendment.

REJECTION OF THE AMENDMENT

The Fourteenth Amendment forced North Carolina politicians to take a stand. Whether the state should ratify it or reject it became the central issue in the state election campaign in 1866. Governor Worth and his followers were strongly opposed to the amendment and wanted the legislature to reject it. They felt that it was degrading the South, and they were angry because it took away the right to vote and hold office from many of the state's former leaders until Congress decided to give back those rights. Some men wondered whether it would even be legal for North Carolina to approve the amendment when representatives of the state had not been allowed to sit in the Congress that proposed it.

Led by the former provisional governor, William Holden, the opponents of the Worth administration decided that they would support the Fourteenth Amendment and the Radical plan of reconstruction. Holden himself had found it hard to support the idea of Negro suffrage in the past, and he still found it hard in the summer of 1866, but early in 1867 he finally came out for it. In September of 1866 Holden's followers met in Raleigh, nominated Alfred Dockery for governor, and called for the approval of the amendment. Holden himself wanted to become governor, but he knew he could not win at this time. He had recently been defeated by Governor Worth, and the Worth administration clearly had the support of a majority of the voters. (Until the adoption of the 1868 Constitution, governors were elected for two-year rather than four-year terms of today.)

In the 1866 election Governor Worth beat Holden's candidate by a majority of over three to one. More important was the fact that the opponents of the Fourteenth Amendment had almost complete control of the legislature. When that body met late in 1866, they turned down the amendment by a vote of 93 to 10 in the House of Commons and 45 to 1 in the Senate.

North Carolina probably could have saved itself a lot of trouble if it had ratified the Fourteenth Amendment in 1866. Tennessee chose to approve it and seemed to satisfy the Radicals. That state did not have to undergo the more extreme plan which the Radicals began to develop after North Carolina and the other southern states turned down the amendment. But the fact remains that the men in the legislature turned down the amendment because they thought it was both illegal and unfair.

THE RECONSTRUCTION ACTS

When North Carolina and the other southern states refused to approve the Fourteenth Amendment, the Radicals in Congress decided that a much stronger and harsher plan of reconstruction was needed. They insisted that the South was being governed by men who were disloyal, that union men were not getting fair treatment in the courts, that the Negroes were still being treated unfairly, and that state and local officials could not maintain law and order. Some of these charges were false, some were true, and some were exaggerated. At any rate Congress decided that the southern states would have to be placed under military rule and used these charges to justify what it was getting ready to do. The result was a series of laws known as the Reconstruction Acts. The first of these acts was passed on March 2, 1867, over the protests and veto of President Johnson. It declared that no legal state government existed in the South and specified that all the southern states besides Tennessee would be put under military control. Five military districts, with a major general in control of each, were to be created. Then the acts described how the new reconstruction process would work. There had to be a convention in each state to draw up new state constitutions. These constitutions had to give the right to vote to all males over twenty-one years old who had lived in their voting district one year and had not had their voting rights taken away from them for taking part on the Confederate side in the Civil War. This meant that Negroes would be allowed to join in the work of reconstruction, but that those white men who had held public office before the war and then aided the Confederacy could not serve in the constitutional conventions or vote for members of the conventions. In North Carolina people like Zebulon B. Vance, the war governor, and William A. Graham, the outstanding leader of the old Whig party, were out of politics for a while because of the amendment.

There were basically two steps in the new method of reconstruction. First the states had to write their new constitutions and have them approved by Congress. Then the state legislatures had to ratify the Fourteenth Amendment. When these two steps were completed Congress would allow representatives from the southern states to take their seats. North Carolina would be back in the union as soon as it performed the duties required by Congress. But first there had to be military rule.

GENERAL SICKLES

North Carolina was under military rule from March, 1867, to July, 1868. During that time the regular state government continued to operate, but it was clearly understood that the final power was in the hands of the major general who commanded the Second Military District. The legislature which was supposed to meet in the fall of 1867 did not assemble.

Before the period of military rule was over two different major generals had been in command of the state. The first of these was Daniel E. Sickles, who is sometimes remembered because he had lost his right leg at Gettysburg and had it pickled so he could proudly display it to his friends. The rule of Sickles was not very harsh, and he usually cooperated with Governor Worth. In most cases the governor was allowed to appoint men to state offices which became vacant, although Sickles could have made the appointments. Some of the rules the general made were kind and generous. For example, he gave people more time to pay their debts, said that no one's home could be taken away from him, would not allow adults to be whipped as a punishment for crimes, and eliminated the death penalty for some offenses. But some of the things Sickles did offended North Carolinians who did not approve of the congressional plan of reconstruction and military rule. They did not like it when he set up military courts in the state and tried civilians in them. Governor Worth

General Daniel E. Sickles was cooperative in his attitude during the period of his command while North Carolina was under military rule. From Francis Trevelyan Miller (editor-in-chief), *The Photographic History of the Civil War in Ten Volumes* (New York: The Review of Reviews Co., 1911), X, 181.

complained about the military courts and was upset when General Sickles ordered that Negroes be allowed to serve on juries.

General Sickles began to carry out the plan of reconstruction by allowing Governor Worth to recommend the names of the men who would register the voters for the coming election. At that point President Johnson removed General Sickles from command of the Second Military District because he had refused to obey an order issued by a federal judge.

GENERAL CANBY

The general who was in charge of North Carolina after the removal of General Sickles was Edwin R. S. Canby. Partly because Canby was a professional soldier instead of a politician like Sickles he did not get along as well with North Carolina leaders as Sickles had. But his policies were not much different from those of Sickles. He continued the military courts and the law which stopped the collection of certain debts. Governor Worth and General Canby got along with each other as well as could be expected, although the governor became very angry when the military authorities arrested the sheriff of Caswell County and took him to Charleston, South Carolina, to be tried before a military commission.

Canby's main job was to supervise the reconstruction of the state according to the plan laid down in the Reconstruction Acts. This he proceeded to do. The voters had been registered by the middle of October, 1867. Then Canby ordered that an election be held in November. The voters would decide first whether or not they wanted to call a constitutional convention. At the same time they would vote for delegates to the convention in case it were called. It was clear that Negroes could not control the election, since there were over 30,000 more whites registered to vote than there were Negroes.

THE REPUBLICAN PARTY

At the time of the convention election in the fall of 1867 there were two clearly divided parties in North Carolina. The older, more established group called itself Conservative, but it might as well have been called the Democratic party. The main reason it did not use that name was that there were many former Whigs in the party who had long opposed the Democrats in state politics. The Whigs and Democrats were now forced to work together in an effort to defeat congressional reconstruction. They wanted North Carolina to be more like it had been before the war, not to change so fast, not to have northern ideas and Negro equality forced on the state.

The party which came out against the Conservatives and for congressional reconstruction and the Negroes called itself the Republican party. The party was officially organized at Raleigh in March, 1867. Its outstanding leader was William W. Holden, who by this time had changed his mind and his party connection so many times that people had lost track of it all. The largest element in the party probably was the Negroes. They were

12

Republicans because the Republican party had ended slavery, and they had been given rights by the Republicans that they had not had before. The Freedmen's Bureau and an organization known as the Union League also helped to instruct the Negroes about politics and insure that they would become and remain loyal Republicans.

There were about as many white men in the Republican party as there were Negroes. Most of these were natives of North Carolina. Some of them were people who had always been opposed to the kind of men who were Conservatives, people who had less education and less wealth than their neighbors. Others were intelligent, educated men who could see that the freeing of the slaves had changed North Carolina's whole way of life and that things could never be the same as they had been before the war. There were Republicans who were interested in rebuilding the state's economic system but realized that it would help if they could get men from the North to invest in railroads and factories. Finally, these men believed that the whites and Negroes should try to be friendly and helpful to each other, and that it just did not make good sense to oppose what Congress was doing to the state. The Conservatives called the native white supporters of the Republican party "scalawags," and the name has stuck. (The origin of the name is not clear, but it probably came from a word first used to describe undersized cattle.)

The group in the Republican party which the Conservatives disliked the most, but which was quite important during the early years of reconstruction, was the carpetbaggers. These were men who had come to the South after the war, some of them carrying their belongings in suitcases made out of carpet cloth. Like all men, some of the carpetbaggers were good and some were bad. Some wanted to help North Carolina while others were more interested in helping themselves. Certainly the carpetbaggers had much influence on the reconstruction of the state. They probably would have had more if they had not sometimes competed with the native whites instead of cooperating with them.

CONVENTION ELECTION OF 1867

In the campaign to decide whether a convention should be called and to elect delegates to it, the Conservatives were not well organized and were confident of victory. Many Conservatives were so disgusted by this time that they simply stayed at home

Albion W. Tourgée, in a sketch done by fourteen-year-old O. Henry, is shown as he left Greensboro for Raleigh. The cartoon appeared on the cover of the Autumn, 1963, issue of the *North Carolina Historical Review;* it was reproduced from a mat supplied by the *Winston-Salem Journal and Sentinel.*

on election day. The result of the election was that the convention was approved by a vote of nearly three to one, with 107 of the 120 delegates being Republicans. Eighteen white carpetbaggers were chosen to go to the convention, along with fifteen Negroes. This means of course that a large majority of the convention were native white North Carolinians.

THE CONSTITUTION OF 1868

The Constitutional Convention of 1868 was in session from the middle of January to the middle of March. Since it drew up a new Constitution that has been used, with some changes, down to the present time, it was one of the most important gatherings in the history of the state. Some historians have been critical of the convention, but at the time it was meeting it was even more harshly denounced. The editor of the leading Conservative newspaper described the convention as "Ham Radicalism in Its Glory." The fact that the delegates did not have much political experience, that some of them were Negroes who did not know much about making laws, and that the carpetbaggers were writing provisions into the Constitution that seemed to fit their home states better than they fitted North Carolina were all pointed out by the critics. The convention cost more than it should have, and when it was over the delegates had a celebration that was wilder than it should have been.

Still, the convention ought to be judged mainly by the work it produced, and this was highly commendable. The old Constitution, written in 1776 and amended in 1835, was badly outdated. The convention now brought North Carolina up to date or at least laid the groundwork for progress in the future.

The Constitution made changes in all three departments of state government, the executive, the legislative, and the judicial. The executive department was changed by adding new offices, including a superintendent of public instruction, a superintendent of public works, and a lieutenant governor. These officials and the governor would now serve for four years instead of two. All of them would be elected by the people instead of chosen by the legislature or some other way. The major executive officers were to serve as an advisory council to the governor. The governor was given the power to shorten the sentences of convicted criminals instead of facing the choice of keeping them in prison for their whole terms or letting them go completely free.

The Constitution made several changes in the lawmaking, or legislative department. The lower house had formerly been called the House of Commons; afterward it was to be called the House of Representatives. The Senate was changed in a more important way. Up to 1868 senators had been chosen on the basis of the wealth of their districts; that is, the parts of the state which had the greatest wealth elected more senators than the poorer areas. The Constitution of 1868 said that the areas having the most people would elect most of the senators, whether they were wealthy or poor. The lieutenant governor would be the president of the senate, instead of allowing the senators to elect their own presiding officer. All senators and representatives had to swear to uphold and defend the national constitution and government.

There were several important provisions in the Constitution concerning the way in which the legislature could raise, spend,

The first and last pages of the Constitution of 1868 are from *North Carolina Documents, 1584-1868*, published by the State Department of Archives and History. The facsimile in the set of documents was reproduced from the original Constitution in the custody of the Secretary of State.

and appropriate money. These provisions were quite important in helping to understand the later history of reconstruction. The state was not allowed to finance any railroads unless they were already being built or unless the state stood to lose money if it did not back up a certain railroad; the only way the legislature could support a new railroad was to get a special vote of approval from the people of the state. If the state went deeper into debt the legislature was supposed to raise a special tax to pay the interest on the new debt. The tax on people, or capitation tax, could never be more than $2.00 a person.

The biggest and probably the most important changes in state government made by the Constitution of 1868 were in the judicial, or court, system. Since the Colonial period the county courts had had great power both in making and enforcing local and state laws. The lawmaking power at the county level was transferred to boards of county commissioners elected by the people. More cases would now be tried before the Superior Courts, and because of this the number of judges was increased from eight to twelve. The Supreme Court was to have five members. Judges could no longer expect to keep their positions for life but had to run for reelection every eight years. Other officers connected with the court system, such as sheriffs and clerks, were also to be elected by the people. They had formerly been appointed by the county courts. All these changes added up to the fact that the people would have more choice of the men who governed them than they had had before.

Many of the provisions in the Constitution were not concerned with the machinery of government but were designed to guarantee a better life for the people of the state. Probably the most important of this type were the sections dealing with the educational system. The state was supposed to establish and maintain a public school system, free of tuition and open to everyone between six and twenty-one years old. The University of North Carolina was to be part of and work closely with the state school system. The schools were supposed to be open on an equal basis to both Negroes and whites. The Constitution also provided that criminals should be reformed as well as punished, and it opened up greater opportunities for people who desired to be elected to a public office.

Almost exactly a hundred years after the close of the constitutional convention, in March, 1968, Governor Dan Moore appointed a commission to study the Constitution of 1868. It has been changed through the years, and will probably be overhauled in the future, but its influence on the state will long remain.

ELECTION OF 1868

After the constitutional convention there was an election in April, 1868, to elect new state and national officers and to see whether or not the voters would approve the new Constitution. It was a bitter campaign, hard fought by both sides. The basic issues were whether the Republicans would be able to take over the state government and whether the Conservatives could defeat a constitution they felt was being forced upon them by carpetbaggers, Negroes, and a Radical Congress.

The Republicans stood solidly in favor of the Constitution and all it represented. They nominated candidates for all the important state offices and Congress. Holden was their choice for governor. After almost three years of waiting for this opportunity, the odds were now all in his favor. It was certain that almost all the Negroes would vote for him, and he could count on the carpetbaggers and many native whites too.

The Conservatives were determined to defeat the new Constitution. There were several provisions in it which they found distasteful. They did not believe the Negroes should be given the right to vote; they wanted the senate based on wealth instead of numbers of people; and they did not like the idea of having judges elected by the people every eight years. The Constitution, they thought, should have forbidden marriages between people of different races and mixing of the races in the public schools and the state university. It was at this time that the Conservatives began to think that they should become the "white man's party." They wanted to run Zeb Vance for governor, but he declined and Thomas S. Ashe became the Conservative candidate.

In the election Holden easily defeated Ashe. The Republicans also won six of the seven seats in Congress. The voters approved the new Constitution by about the same majority that Holden had won over Ashe. Some voters apparently felt that if they went out and defeated the Constitution, Congress would just think up an even harder plan of reconstruction, and North Carolina would have to wait much longer to get back in the union. If all the Conservatives had voted they probably could have elected Ashe and defeated the Constitution.

HOLDEN TAKES POWER

William W. Holden gave his inaugural address on the fourth of July, 1868. Then he went to the governor's office to get the keys from Governor Worth, who was upset and angry because he had been forced out of his position by Congress and a military

Governor Holden's Raleigh home was located on the corner of Hargett and McDowell streets where the Professional Building now stands. From Duke University Library.

order from General Canby. Before Worth left his office he protested his removal, saying that Holden's election was not legal. After that he walked outside, looked around for his horse (which he afterward found), and said, "They have taken my pony too."

About the time Holden became the regular governor he called a special session of the legislature to ratify the Fourteenth Amendment. This was done on July 2. At that point General Canby declared that the federal troops in the state would no longer interfere with the state government. Within three weeks after these events Congress allowed the representatives and senators from North Carolina to take their seats. North Carolina was back in the union. It had been over seven years since the state seceded.

THE REPUBLICAN LEGISLATURE

The Republicans controlled the legislature only from 1868 to 1870, but this was long enough to earn them a very bad reputation among the historians of North Carolina. It has been described as a time of "bad government" and a time of "pillage and plunder." The main criticism of the legislature was the way it mismanaged the state's money, and especially the manner in which the railroads secured money from the taxpayers with the approval of the legislature. This is how it worked. A railroad would ask the state for help. Most of them were in bad condition as a result of the war, and there was general agreement that they needed state aid. The legislature would then issue state bonds to raise money for the railroads. The railroads sold the bonds themselves. The money from the sale of bonds was supposed to be used for building railroads, and for no other purpose.

Supporting the railroads was basically a sound thing to do, but the politicians and some businessmen soon began to take advantage of it to make personal profits and in other ways to further their own interests. Altogether the Convention of 1868 and the Republican legislatures of 1868 and 1869 approved the issue of about $28 million in bonds. Of the bonds that were actually issued the largest part went to three railroads, the Western North Carolina, the Chatham, and the Wilmington, Charlotte and Rutherford.

The issue of so many bonds soon began to damage North Carolina's good credit. Men began to wonder whether the state would ever be able to pay back what the bonds promised to pay; as a result the price of the bonds dropped and the state had to issue more bonds to raise the money the railroads needed.

Another serious complaint about the railroad bonds was that they were unconstitutional. The Constitution said that the state could not issue new bonds when they were selling for less than the amount they promised to pay the holder unless a special tax was levied to pay the interest. When the legislature levied these special taxes they were taxing the people of the state more heavily than the Constitution allowed. The lawmakers also violated the Constitution by supporting new railroads without getting the approval of the people in special elections.

It was bad enough that the legislature had violated the Constitution, but even worse was the fact that some of the members were involved in activities that were fraudulent. To be more exact, some of the members sold their votes for large sums of money. The main villain in the story was a New York carpetbagger named Milton S. Littlefield. Called at the time General Littlefield, he has since been dubbed the "Prince of Carpetbaggers." Certainly he made enough money from his illegal schemes to live like a prince. Most of this money came to him from a businessman named George W. Swepson, a native of North Carolina who had been appointed by Governor Holden as president of the Western Division of the North Carolina Railroad. Swepson would give the money to Littlefield and Littlefield then used it to buy votes. He also did a number of special favors for important members of the legislature. Some of them got

This close-up of steps in the State Capitol shows broken places which tradition says were caused by barrels of whiskey being rolled down the steps during the Reconstruction period. Until contemporary evidence is found, the story must be accepted as an exaggeration of the "excesses" of the Reconstruction legislature.

bonds, others got fine meals, and any of them could get alcoholic drinks from a bar set up in the west wing of the Capitol building. Persons both outside and in the legislature profited from these illegal and fraudulent activities.

The corruption and some of the extravagance that went along with it did not last very long. After about a year some of the Republicans and most of the Conservatives began to discover what had been going on, and a carpetbagger from Craven County, W. H. S. Sweet, asked for an investigation. The only result was that one of the Conservative members was caught taking money he should not have accepted. Later investigations by special investigating commissions learned most of the details about the bribery and fraud connected with the sale of railroad bonds.

So much has been written about the unfavorable side of the period of Republican rule that students seldom read about some of the useful and needed things it accomplished. In 1869 the legislature passed a school law which attempted to revive the state's system of public schools, and by the next year the income for the schools was slightly over $150,000. There were several measures which were designed to improve the treatment of criminals. Among these were the abolition of whipping for crimes and the establishment of a penitentiary. Up to this time there had been no state prison. Against the opposition of the Conservatives the legislature provided for the revival of the militia. A whole new code of laws concerning the trial of civil cases was enacted. In an effort to strike at the Ku Klux Klan, it was made a crime to wear a mask or disguise on a public highway for the purpose of frightening a citizen. Early in 1870 the legislature asked Congress to extend a general amnesty

This Ku Klux Klan costume was worn by a member of the Klan in North Carolina in 1870. It is owned by the Buffalo and Erie County Historical Society, Buffalo, New York, which furnished the photograph.

to those people who were still denied certain rights because of their past conduct. Finally, the legislature ratified both the Fourteenth and Fifteenth amendments to the United States Constitution. The Fourteenth Amendment made the Negroes citizens and the Fifteenth said that they should not be denied the right to vote.

Lately some historians have tried to find explanations for the conduct of the Negro-carpetbagger legislatures that controlled the South around 1870 and to justify some of the things they did. They have pointed out that bad government existed in the North as well as in the South during reconstruction. According to them, the Negroes and carpetbaggers wanted to provide more services for the people. These services would cost much more money than the states had ever spent before. That is the reason taxes were higher during reconstruction than they were before the war and immediately after the Reconstruction period. The state governments had been stingy and the people had been against heavy taxes. It has also been pointed out that taxes were not nearly as high then and the governments did not spend nearly as much as they would in the twentieth century. Some historians believe and say that at least some of the carpetbaggers were truly interested in improving the South and in making it a better place to live. The scoundrels like Milton Littlefield were not the most common type of carpetbagger.

Many persons would consider these favorable statements about the Negro-carpetbagger legislatures as excuses for conduct that cannot be justified. Yet most of them are true of North Carolina. The state had not been willing to do much for the people except to maintain law and order. It had begun to provide public schools but not much else. The Negroes and carpetbaggers were saying that the government must do more, and to do this they raised taxes even above the limit they themselves had set. Because most white North Carolinians had long been against increased taxes they were disturbed by what the Republican legislature was doing. Even if the Republicans had given the state good government, had not raised taxes, and had not been involved in corruption, the Conservatives would have been bitterly opposed to them because some of them were black, some were not properly educated, and some of them were from outside the state. To put it another way, the enemies of the Negroes, scalawags, and carpetbaggers opposed them not so much because they governed bady, but because they were in the positions of power which the old Whigs and Democrats had divided between themselves. At any rate the Conservatives were determined to put the Negro back "in his place," chase out the carpetbaggers, and remove from power the scalawag William Holden and his friends.

JOSIAH TURNER'S ROLE

Perhaps the most determined of the Conservatives and the one who helped more than any other single person to throw the Republicans out of power was the editor of the Raleigh *Sentinel*,

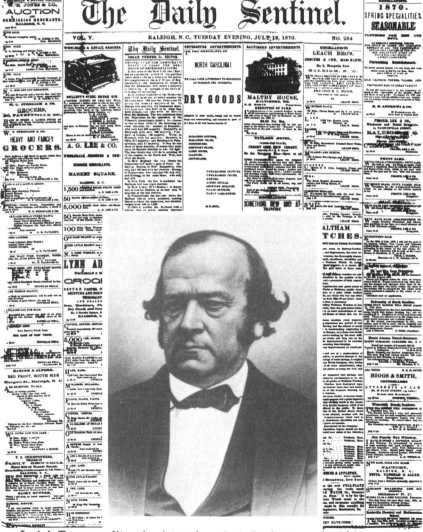

Josiah Turner, editor, is pictured against the front page of his newspaper for July 19, 1870.

Josiah Turner, Jr. He had a sharp tongue and one of the bitterest pens that ever wrote editorials for a North Carolina newspaper. Hating the Republicans and all they stood for, he attacked them both personally and as a party. One of his favorite methods was to call the Republicans by unflattering nicknames. Some of these were "Chicken," "Grapevine," "Parson," "Blow your Horn Billy," and "Greasy Sam." He referred to Governor Holden as a "white-livered miscreant" and said that the carpetbaggers had turned North Carolina into a "hog trough." While the legislature was in session, Turner kept a close watch on all its proceedings, denounced what it was doing, and exposed anything that appeared to him corrupt. If the story of reconstruction were turned into a play, Turner would have to be cast in the role of the hero of the white men and the Conservative party.

THE KU KLUX KLAN

Almost as colorful as Josiah Turner, and just as important in the effort to get rid of the Negroes and their friends, was the organization called the Ku Klux Klan. It was a secret society of white men which had sprung up in Tennessee just after the war and had spread into North Carolina by late 1867 or early 1868. After it became active in politics in 1868, it grew larger and more active down to about 1871 and then dwindled away after the Conservatives regained control of the state legislature. The Klan had several excuses for its existence. In the first place, the Republicans had a secret organization of their own, the Union League. It controlled the Negroes, making sure that they stood firmly behind the Republican party. Some members of the Klan felt that white women needed to be protected from Negro men, or at least that Negro men who became too friendly with white women should be punished severely. Another reason the Klan existed was that the Negro seemed to be going too far and too fast—they would have said he was getting "uppity" and had to be kept down, not in slavery of course but in a low social position. But the work which interested the Klan most of all was that of weakening the Republican party. To do this they were willing to resort to any method, either legal or illegal.

The Klan in North Carolina had an elaborate and strange organization headed by Colonel William L. Saunders, a prominent resident of Chapel Hill. The state leader was called the Grand Dragon, and the chief officer in a district was the Grand Titan. In the various communities there were units called dens, each headed by the Grand Cyclops; the dens in a county were

The Ku Klux Klan costumes were drawn from a photograph made in 1868 by Federal soldiers who captured the costumes after a Klan parade. The picture is owned by the Department of History of Louisiana State University in Baton Rouge, Louisiana; it was reproduced by the Duke University Library.

under the control of an officer called either the Grand Mogul or the Grand Giant. Although most people picture in their minds the Klan members riding about in long white robes, masks, and pointed caps with horns, there was considerable variety in the costumes. Some of the pictures one sees of Klan members are not really Klan members at all, but are members of the Consitutional Union Guard or of the White Brotherhood, two organizations very much like the Klan. The Klan robes were sometimes red, although they were more commonly white, and they had more decorations than those of the other organizations. The White Brotherhood wore horns, probably to make the Negroes think they were devils. Sometimes men belonged to all three of the secret organizations. They might go on a Klan raid one night and a White Brotherhood raid the next night; on both occasions they would wear the same costume.

Regardless of what the members wore, the Ku Klux Klan spread terror wherever it went. Its punishments ranged all the way from threats and whippings to the most brutal murders. Most of the victims were Negroes, but it was not uncommon for white men who had helped a Negro or been friendly in some way to be visited by the Klan. It is frequently stated that the Klan was punishing people for being criminals or taking part in immoral acts, but this is not true. Most of their victims were Negroes who were doing things they had not been formerly allowed to do, such as eating with whites or talking back to a white man or carrying a gun. Negroes were whipped or even killed for taking part in politics. The Klan wanted people to believe that the Negroes were responsible for most of the crimes in the state and that they could not be dealt with in the courts because the Freedmen's Bureau was protecting the black men and most of the judges in the state courts were Republicans. The Conservatives and Klansmen insisted that Judge Tourgée, in particular, the Ohio carpetbagger who had helped write the state Constitution, was partial to the Negroes in his court, but the man who knows the most about Judge Tourgée, his biographer, Otto H. Olsen, has shown clearly that this was not true.

What this all adds up to is that none of the excuses the Klan used to justify its actions will stand up under a close examination. Certainly the women of North Carolina were in no great danger, and the Union League was not a band of criminals. One is led to believe, then, that the Ku Klux Klan was mainly a political organization which covered its actions with excuses in the same way they covered their bodies when they made their visits. There are several facts which would seem to prove that the Klan was more interested in politics than in anything else. It grew in strength as soon as the Republicans came into power and disappeared soon after the Conservatives regained control of the legislature. It is also noteworthy that the two counties where the Klan was engaged in its worst terrorism, Alamance and Caswell, were about the only counties in the state where the Republican party had gained strength in the fall elections of 1868. The Klan operated mostly in the parts of the state where it had a fair chance of beating the Negroes in the political wars; there was not much Klan activity in the counties which had a large majority of Negroes. When a man joined the Klan he had to take an oath which said, in part: "I reject and oppose the principles of the radical party." Because of this oath, and for other reasons too, nearly all the Klan members belonged to the Conservative party. Some members of the state legislature even belonged to the Klan. It is revealing too that a number of Republican leaders were murdered by the Klan, while there is no record of a Conservative politician's being killed because of his political beliefs.

Whatever else one may say or feel about the Ku Klux Klan, it is clear that it sprang from the conditions that marked the post-Civil War era, and especially the period of Radical reconstruction. If times had not been hard, if Congress had not tried to give the Negroes more of an equal place, if the carpetbaggers had stayed at home, and if the Republican party had never come into power, the Ku Klux Klan would not have come into being. But the fact remains that those conditions did exist, and those people of North Carolina who preferred to keep things the way they had been before could believe that terrorism and murder might help them save the state from all its agony.

THE KIRK-HOLDEN WAR

The Klan was a threat to the Republican party and to the personal power of Governor Holden almost from the time it became active in North Carolina. The Republicans had befriended the Negroes and had to have their votes to stay in power. If the black voters could be frightened out of politics it was almost certain that the Conservatives would come back into power in the election of 1870. There were other reasons too why Holden and the Republican legislature felt they had to do something about the Klan. It was the duty of the governor to maintain law and order in the state and to see that every citizen, black and white, was protected in his rights and in his person. The state simply could not allow men to take the law into their own hands and go around hanging and shooting people.

Late in 1869 the legislature passed a law called the Shoffner Act. Basically, this law did two things. It said that the governor could put any county in the state under martial law whenever he decided that the county officers could not keep law and order. The Shoffner Act also made it possible for anyone who was being tried for wearing a mask, murder, or conspiracy to have the scene of his trial transferred to a county other than the one in which the crime had occurred. The legislators apparently believed that it would be impossible to convict a Klan member in his own county, and it probably would have been.

The climax of the events in William Holden's struggle with the Klan and the acts which soon led to the governor's downfall came in 1870 after the Klan murdered or plotted the murder of two Republican leaders in Alamance and Caswell counties. The first victim was Wyatt Outlaw, an outstanding Negro in Alamance County, one of the men who helped organize the Republican party in North Carolina, and a former president of the local Union League. Near midnight, late in February, the Klan surrounded the town of Graham, dragged Outlaw to the town square, and hanged him from a sturdy oak tree near the county courthouse.

The second murder was more important because it finally moved Governor Holden to action. This time the Klan's target was John W. Stephens, who is usually remembered by the nickname, "Chicken." The trouble with Stephens, so far as the Klan was concerned, was that he had been too successful as a Republican politician and that he had too much influence with the Negroes. To strike back at the Klan for its actions, some of the Negroes began burning barns, and the Klan insisted that Stephens not only had encouraged them to do the burning but had also provided them with matches. Here, in the words of the historian of reconstruction in North Carolina, J. D. de Roulhac Hamilton, is what happened to Stephens:

In March, 1870, a large Conservative meeting was held in Yanceyville. Stephens was present taking notes upon a speech of Judge Kerr when he was requested to come down stairs for a few moments. In company with the person making the request, he walked down stairs, through the corridor which was crowded with people listing taxes, and went into an unoccupied office. Instantly, seven men seized him, and his companion departed closing the door after him, leaving Stephens tightly held. After three seven-shot revolvers had been taken from him, he was bound, gagged, and laid upon a pile of wood in the corner. One man, left to keep guard, stretched out on the hearth in order that the negroes who thronged the square on which the windows opened might not see him, and the other six left and walked down the corridor to Judge Kerr's office, which was unoccupied during its owner's speech upstairs. The original plan had been to keep Stephens until night and then to hang him in the square, but the danger of discovery was so great that it was now decided not to delay at all. Walking back through the crowd, they re-entered the room and cut his throat, at the same time drawing a rope tightly about his neck, and stabbed him to the heart, after which they left. The provocation was undoubtedly great, but few can deny the horror of the punishment. His body was not discovered until the next day and, while the Ku Klux were at once suspected, no evidence could be secured.

The statement of John G. Lea relates details concerning the murder of John W. Stephens. The original statement is in the State Archives, State Department of Archives and History; it is reproduced on this and the following page and a half.

The North Carolina Historical Commission
OFFICE OF THE SECRETARY
RALEIGH

July 2, 1919.

At the request of the North Carolina Historical Commission, I have written the true story of the events of the Reconstruction Period in this State, which centered mainly at Yanceyville in Caswell County, where the killing of the notorious, John W. Stevens, took place in the courthouse. I have given all the facts of which I have full knowledge as a participant in the stirring events of that time.

John G. Lea

Witness to the reading of the story and to this signature. Fred. A. Olds.

Immediately after the surrender of General Lee, in April, 1865, a bummer named Albion W. Tourgee, of New York, from Sherman's army, came to Caswell County and organized a Union League, and they were drilling every night and beating the drums, and he made many speeches telling the negroes that he was sent by the government and that he would see that they got forty acres of land. He succeeded in getting J. W. Stevens and Jim Jones appointed justices of the peace of Caswell County and they annoyed the farmers very much by holding court every day, persuading the darkies to warrant the farmer, &c. Stevens was run out of Rockingham County for stealing a chicken.

The first trial that Jim Jones had, a negro stole Captain Mitchell's hog. He was caught cleaning the hog by Mitchell's son and by a darky whose name was Paul McGee. He was carried before Jones and Jones turned him loose and said he had been appointed by Governor Holden to protect the negro and that he intended to do it. Soon thereafter I formed the Ku Klux Klan and was elected county organiser. I organized a den in every township in the county and the Ku Klux whipped Jones and drove him out of the county.

J. W. Stevens burned the hotel in Yanceyville and a row of brick stores. He also burned Gen. William Lee's entire crop of tobacco, and Mr. Sam Hinton's crop. Ed. Slade, a darky, told that he burned the barn of tobacco by an order of Stevens and another darky told about his burning the hotel, also by an order. Stevens was tried by the Ku Klux Klan and sentenced to death. He had a fair trial before a jury of twelve men. At a democratic convention he approached exsheriff Wiley and tried to get him to run on the republican ticket for sheriff. Wiley said he would let him know that day. He came to me and informed me of that fact and suggested that he would fool him into that room in which he was killed. He did so and ten or twelve men went into the room and he was found dead

next morning. A democratic convention was in session in the court room on the second floor of the courthouse in Yanceyville, to nominate county officers and members of the Legislature. Mr. Wiley, who was in the convention, brought Stevens down to a rear room on the ground floor, then used for the storage of wood for the courthouse. I had ordered all the Ku Klux Klan in the county to meet at Yanceyville that day, with their uniforms under their saddles, and they were present. Mr. Wiley came to me and suggested that it would be a better plan, as Stevens had approached him to run on the republican ticket for sheriff and he had told him that he would let him know that day, to fool him down stairs, and so just before the convention closed, Wiley beckoned to Stevens and carried him down stairs, and Captain Mitchell, James Denny and Joe Fowler went into the room and Wiley came out. Mitchell proceeded to disarm him (he had three pistols on his body). He soon came out and left Jim Denny with a pistol at his head and went to Wiley and told him that he couldn't kill him himself. Wiley came to me and said "You must do something; I am exposed unless you do." Immediately I rushed into the room, with eight or ten men, found him sitting flat on the floor. He arose and approached me and we went and sat down where the wood had been taken away, in an opening in the wood on the wood-pile, and he asked me not to let them kill him. Captain Mitchell rushed at him with a rope, drew it around his neck, put his feet against his chest and by that time about a half dozen men rushed up: Tom Oliver, Pink Morgan, Dr. Richmond and Joe Fowler. Stevens was then stabbed in the breast and also in the neck by Tom. Oliver, and the knife was thrown at his feet and the rope left around his neck. We all came out, closed the door and locked it on the outside and took the key and threw it into County Line Creek. I may add that it was currently believed that Stevens murdered his mother while living with him. Stevens kept his house, within sight of the courthouse

and now standing, in a state of war all the time with doors and windows barred with iron bars and a regular armory with a large supply of ammunition.

Col. A. K. McClure of Philadelphia, Pa., came to Yanceyville. He was for Horace Greely against Grant. Wilson Cary, a colored man, better known as the "Archives of Gravity" replied to Col. McClure and said that Senator Stevens, who had been elected to the State Senate by the negroes, stole a chicken and was sent to the State Senate and if he would steal a gobbler he would be sent to Congress, and you could have heard the negroes yell for miles around and there were at least 2000 negroes present.

The first state election we had in North Carolina, when Gov. Holden was elected, we had 2800 negro majority. The Freedmen's Bureau Agent from Michigan, Captain Dawes, came down to take charge of the election. I carried him down home with me. He and I fought each other in the Civil War. I carried him out fox hunting and had a beautiful chase, and on the day of election he came to me and said that he was sent to carry the election by the government and if it was found out on him he would be courtmartialed and possibly shot. He told me where he put the ballot box, so I worked on the ballot box until twelve o'clock at night and then rode to Locust Hill, nine miles distant, and counted until day, and we elected a ticket by twenty-seven votes. Caswell's bonds stood at par, while Person and Rockingham, adjoining counties, went down to five and six dollars. They went Republican.

To show the feeling, I may say, at the first State election after the War, in 1866, Tom Lea, colored, voted the democratic ticket. A great mob of negroes gathered in Yanceyville and we learned that they had seized him. There were hundreds in the mob, and when we came up

we found that they had Tom on a rail and were carrying him around, sing-
ing and shouting as they went. With me were Sheriff Griffith, Thos. L.
Lea and Weldon Price. We rushed upon the crowd and the sheriff struck
several of the mob and knocked them down and we took Tom from then, un-
hurt.

      Governor Holden was born in Caswell County and knew the situ-
ation. That was why he was so prejudiced against the county. He declared
martial law and had every prominent citizen arrested by a regiment of cut
throats, who could neither read nor write, from western North Carolina
and eastern Tennessee, commanded by Col. Geo. W. Kirk. Col. George
Williamson got a writ of habeas corpus from Judge Mitchell of Salisbury,
but Col. Kirk and Governor Holden did not obey it. He then went to
Chief Justice Pearson, with the same result. I then came to Raleigh with
Col. Williamson and saw General Matt. W. Ransom and told him of our troubles and he said that he would go that night to Elizabeth City and see
Judge Brooks, U. S. District Judge. He issued the writ, and we went back
to Danville. Captain Graves and Col. Williamson served the writ. Lt.
Colonel Burgin of Kirk's regiment told Colonel Williamson that if he
ever put his foot in Yanceyville again he would shoot his head off.
They failed to arrest me on the day of the general arrest, so I went home
and the next day they came and arrested me and brought me to Raleigh.
Major Yates came to my house with ten or twelve men and when he came
to the house I was lying down, asleep. It was raining, and my sisters
came running into the house and told me there was a crowd of Kirk's
men out in the yard. I rushed to a drawer and got my pistols, but
my sister grabbed me and told me not to go out in the yard nor to try to
use my pistols. The major came to the door and said: "I come to arrest

you and take you to Raleigh as a witness". I said, "By what authority
do you make this arrest", and he said "by authority of the Governor of
the State". I told him that I could not walk to Yanceyville, seven
miles distant. He told me to have my horse sent up to the church that
he had more prisoners up there. When I arrived at the church. Lil
Graves, a colored man, said: "Mars' John, I didn't bring them. They
made me come. They have sent Mars' Nat on". They sent me with one
man, a youth of 24, with a rifle slung at his back, on an old horse
twenty-four years old belonging to Dr. Garner, while I was on my
speedy fox hunting mare. I could have made my escape easily but on
account of my younger brother I thought it best for me to go. When I
got to Yanceyville. to my surprise I found my brother in great glee,
laughing. I asked him what was the matter. He said that a thrashing
machine had just come into town and Kirk's men thought it was a cannon
and they rushed into the courthouse and grabbed their guns. The soldier
that carried me begged me all the way to Yanceyville not to let anybody
shoot him. He also asked me to let him get behind me. He then unslung
his gun and so we went into the town. This guard begged me to let him
come to my house and work for me, saying he did not expect to find so many
kind people and that he would be glad to live in the neighborhood; that
he had been brought down from the mountains, not knowing where he was
going nor what he was to do, or what sort of people he would be among.
When Kirk's men arrived in Yanceyville, Old Aunt Millie Lee was selling
ice cream at the courthouse. It was the first they had ever seen and
several of them said "Ain't this the best frozen victuals you ever tast-

      A man by the name of John Spellman, editor of a Raleigh paper
went to Governor Holden and had me released on my own recognizance. I

then went over to the hotel at Raleigh and found Judge Kerr, Col. Williamson, Sam Hill and others. Judge Kerr advised me to take the first train
out and go to Arkansas, saying if I stayed here they would hang me. I
told him that I had two uncles living near Little Rock, Ark., who came to
my father's every summer and they looked so much like a corpse that I was
like General Grant, "I believe I had rather be hung here than die of slow
fever in Arkansas". So the next day they arrested Capt. Mitchell, Sheriff
Wiley, Felix Roan and myself and tried us before the Supreme judges, Dick,
Settle and Pearson. The trial lasted for a week. Ex-Governor Bragg and
Judge Battle defended us. Bailey and Badger prosecuted and they never did
prove that there was a Ku Klux Klan in Caswell County.

      The day that Kirk arrived in Yanceyville I went to Judge Bowe
and said to him that there were enough ex-confederate soldiers there to
whip Kirk's regiment and Judge Bowe said that that would never do, that
we had better go into the court room, where the candidates were speaking.
We went and he took his seat inside the bar. I sat down behind him. Col.
Kirk marched his men, four abreast, up the steps. He walked in front of
Bowe and asked if this was Bowe. Bowe told him it was. He said "I arrest
you". Judge Bowe asked him by what authority. With an oath he shook his
pistol at him and said "By this", whereupon Judge Bowe shoved him back
and told him that was no order. I had a large hickory stick in my hand.
I raised the stick to hit him, when Tobe Williamson caught it and kept
me from striking him, and you had better believe I was glad he did. I
left Yanceyville that evening and went over to Danville and got the writ
of habeas corpus as above stated.

      The day I was arrested I was carried to Yanceyville and all the
prisoners had been sent over to Graham except a few from Alamance who had
confessed being Ku Klux. I was carried over to Graham the next day and
all the other Caswell boys started to Raleigh next morning. Late

that afternoon Judge James Boyd, United States Judge, came and asked me
how I would like to take a walk; that he had permission to take me out
provided I would agree to come back. I agreed, so we walked awhile, finally coming to his house. He asked me to have a seat on the porch. In
a few minutes the bell rang for supper. I told him I had plenty to eat at
the courthouse, that my friends had sent in to me, Mr. Banks Holt and
others, but he insisted on my taking a warm supper and as soon as we finished eating he said to me, "Lea, I was a Ku Klux. I have disgraced myself and my little wife". I asked him how. "I turned State's evidence".
Why did you do it? He replied "Moral cowardice. When Kirk's men hung
Murray up by the neck and they let him down he was apparently dead (he
lived 20 years after this, but really died from the effects of this in-
jury), they then came to me and put the rope around my neck and I wilted".
He and his young wife both cried like a baby and Boyd said. "Lea, I will
never expose you. I know you are the county commander in Caswell". I
said, "Oh no, there are a great many Leas in Caswell; I am not the one".

      The day the arrest was made in Yanceyville, late that afternoon,
Lt. Col. Burgin with eight men went down after ex-sheriff Wiley, nine miles
from Yanceyville; went in his tobacco field where he was standing and told
him they had come to arrest him. He asked them by what authority. Burgin
shook his pistol at him and said, with an oath, "This is my authority".
His men rushed on Wiley, who knocked down seven of them, but one slipped
up behind him with a fence rail and knocked him down; they then put Wiley
on a horse, bare-back, tied his feet to the horse and whipped him nearly
all the way to Yanceyville. The blood flowed freely, he being in his
shirt sleeves. Burgin told me that Wiley was the bravest man he ever saw.
When they arrived in Yanceyville, that afternoon, Burgin took him into a
room in the courthouse, ordered his men to draw their guns on him, and told

him that if he did not tell who killed Stevens they would kill him.
With his head straight as could be he opened his coat, slapped his chest
and dared them to shoot.

The night I reached Graham they put sheriff Wiley and Josiah
Turner in jail with a crazy negro who holloed all night long. They didn't
sleep a wink. Next morning they were taken out to go to Raleigh and Mr.
Turner kept repeating that the powers of the judiciary were exhausted and
Col. Kirk told him to shut his mouth. He then flapped his arms and crow-
ed like a rooster and said "Well, I reckon I can crow". Kirk then said
"Hush up that, fool". The militia detachment were terribly frightened,
thinking that they would be attacked in Durham. They closed all the windows and barred all the doors.

The night after Jones was whipped the Ku Flux went up to see
if he had moved, having been ordered to do so. There were three very
worthy darkies living in the neighborhood, named Stephen Taylor, William
Garland and Frank Chandler. They were carried up to the grave yard by
the Ku Klux, where we had left our horses. I walked through the grave
yard, placed my hands on Will's naked shoulder and it nearly scared him
to death. He shook all over. The next day Will came by my house and
Capt. Graves, my brother-in-law, asked him where he was going. Will
said, "Lordy, Mars' Billy, I'm going across the creek". "What's the matter, Billy?" asked Capt. Graves. "Dem things got me last night. They
were as tall as the eaves of this house. I knows they came out of the
graves, for I saw them with my own eyes and one came up and put his hand
on my shoulder and his hands chilled me clean through".

While I and the three others referred to were being tried
before the Supreme Court, on the lower floor of the Capitol, on the
bench warrant issued for us, the trial of the prisoners from Caswell
County taken by the writ of Judge Brooks, which was the third writ, was
being held in the Senate Chamber, directly over us. Our case was dis-
missed and we left at once for home. They had a great demonstration in
Raleigh. There was a street Parade, cannon were fired, tar barrels burned and speeches by a great many prominent men were made. Judge Kerr's
speech created great excitement and enthusiasm. Only Wiley and Josiah
Turner went to jail. When I reached home, Sheriff Griffith, who had been
a prisoner, came and summonsed me to go with him and we ordered the heads
of the Union League of America to leave the county within twenty-four
hours and they did so without exception, going to Danville.

John G. Lea submitted a signed statement in 1919 relating to the murder
of Stephens. It was released after Lea's death on September 29, 1935; the
story appeared in newspapers on October 1, 1935.

There are several other facts about the Stephens murder which throw light on the conditions in Caswell County, show what the Republican party was up against in that area, and help to explain why Governor Holden thought it was necessary to send state troops to halt the Klan. The man who lured Stephens to the room where he was killed was the former sheriff of the county, a man respected by his neighbors and supposedly law-abiding. The murderers were themselves prominent men in the community. At least four of them were active in the work of the Conservative party. The central figure in the murder plot, the ex-sheriff, was a member of the Klan, but still the state was not able to collect evidence that the Klan had anything to do with the slaying.

Holden then decided that the only way to deal with the situation in Alamance and Caswell counties was to organize a force of state troops and send it into the area to arrest and try the leaders of the Klan or anyone else who had been involved in the crime and violence there. Holden's critics then and some writers now say that he intended to use the state troops for political purposes. His defenders argued that martial law was the only way to deal with the problem of maintaining order and justice. There is probably some truth in the statements of both Holden's critics and his defenders, but no one will ever know with certainty what went on in the governor's mind as he made his fateful decision to go to war with the Ku Klux Klan.

Holden's first step in his effort to secure order and subdue the Klan was to raise two regiments of state troops. Only one of these was actually used in the exciting events of the summer of 1870. It was under the command of Colonel George W. Kirk, a man many North Carolinians hated intensely because he had been the commander of a regiment of United States troops during the war. By July Kirk had completed his organization, and it was sworn into the service of North Carolina. The Conservatives bitterly denounced Holden and Kirk. Even some of the governor's friends and fellow party members had their doubts that he was doing the right thing by declaring martial law and threatening people.

Kirk soon moved his troops into Alamance and Caswell, taking over the county courthouses and letting it be known that military rule would be enforced. The activity of the Klan came to an end after the soldiers arrived. The soldiers were sometimes rowdy, and people heard them bragging and making threats. There was fear that the people of Caswell and Alamance would

A PROCLAMATION

BY THE GOVERNOR OF NORTH-CAROLINA.

Executive Department,
Raleigh, March 7th, 1870.

By Virtue of Authority, Vested in me by the Constitution of the State, and by virtue of an act passed at the present session of the General Assembly, entitled "An act to secure the better protection of life and property," ratified the 29th day of January, 1870, and for the reason that the civil authorities of the County of Alamance are not able to protect the citizens of said County in the enjoyment of life and property, I hereby proclaim and declare that the County of Alamance is in a state of insurrection.

On the 26th of November, 1869, a citizen of the United States, who was engaged in teaching a school in said County, was taken from his house by a band of men armed and disguised, and was by them cruelly beaten and scourged.

In the night of the 26th of February, 1870, a citizen of said County was taken from his house by a band of men armed and disguised, and was by them hanged by the neck until he was dead on the public square in the town of Graham, near the Court House.

And more recently the Postmaster at Company Shops, in said County, an officer of the Government of the United States, was compelled to flee his County, and while absent a band of men armed and disguised visited his

house, with the purpose, doubtless, of taking his life, and thus within a short distance of Federal troops stationed in said County not to oppress or intimidate good citizens, but to preserve the peace and to protect the innocent and the law-abiding.

In addition to these cases information has been received at this Department that peaceable and law-abiding citizens of the County aforesaid have been molested in their homes, have been whipped, shot, scourged, and threatened with further visitations of violence and outrage unless they would conform to some arbitrary standard of conduct set up by these disguised assassins and murderers.

I have issued proclamation after proclamation to the people of the State, warning offenders and wicked or misguided violators of the law to cease their evil deeds, and, by treating better lives, propitiate those whose duty it is to enforce the law. I have invoked public opinion to aid me in repressing these outrages, used in governing peace and order. I have sought to see if the people of Alamance would reassemble in public meeting and express their condemnation of such conduct by a portion of the citizens of the County, but I have waited in vain. No meeting of the kind has been held. No expression of disapproval even of such conduct by the great body of the citizens has yet reached this Department: but, on the contrary, it is believed that the time of citizens who have repeated these crimes in the Executive have been thereby endangered, and it is further believed that many of the citizens of the County are so terrified that they dare not complain, or attempt the arrest of criminals in their midst. The civil officers of the County are silent and powerless.

The laws must be maintained. These laws are our all. Every citizen, of whatever party or color, must be absolutely free to express his political opinions, and must and SHALL cease. Criminals must and SHALL be brought to justice. The whole power of both governments, State and Federal, is pledged to this, and that power will be exerted. Criminals who may escape to Counties

adjoining Alamance will be pursued, and, if not delivered up by the civil authorities of said Counties, or if sheltered or protected in said Counties with the knowledge of the civil authorities, the said Counties will also be declared to be in a state of insurrection.

I earnestly appeal to all good citizens to aid the civil authorities in maintaining peace and good order, and to support me in my purpose to protect life and property without regard to party or color.

Done at the City of Raleigh, this 7th day of March, 1870, and in the 94th year of our Independence.

W. W. HOLDEN,
Governor.

By the Governor:
W. R. RICHARDSON,
Private Secretary.

The original of Governor William W. Holden's proclamation of March 7, 1870, relating to insurrection in Alamance County is in the Supreme Court file of the case of *Ex Parte Adolphus G. Moore*, 64 N.C. 802 (1870).

become so angry that they would attack the soldiers and a local civil war would follow, but this never came close to happening.

Probably the worst part of the military rule and certainly the part that finally resulted in Holden's downfall was the arrest of eighty-two men in Alamance County and nineteen in Caswell. A military court was set up to try these persons, some of whom were put into jail and not allowed to go free on bail. In some cases the prisoners were not told why they were being put into jail. All the soldiers could tell them was that they were acting under orders from Colonel Kirk, who in turn was acting under orders from Governor Holden.

In the American system of justice a prisoner who thinks he is being held unjustly may apply for a legal paper called in lawyer's language a writ of habeas corpus, which means literally "to have the body." The writ is issued by a judge, and it orders whoever is holding the prisoner in jail to bring the prisoner before the judge, who then can decide whether the prisoner is being held illegally. The right of habeas corpus is one of the most basic of all human rights because it can be and has been used to protect persons from rulers who are trying to exercise more authority than they have under the law. By issuing a writ of habeas corpus a judge can become a hero in a struggle for freedom against a king or a president or a state governor. By refusing to issue the writ a judge can become the villain. As it turned out in the story of North Carolina during reconstruction the judges proved to be both heroes and villains.

In the middle of July, 1870, one of the prisoners in Alamance County, A. G. Moore, applied for a writ of habeas corpus to the chief justice of the state Supreme Court, Richmond M. Pearson. His lawyers were leading Conservative politicians, including William A. Graham, Thomas Bragg, and Augustus S. Merrimon. It clearly was a contest now between the Conservative party and Governor Holden, with the chief justice caught in the middle. When Moore's lawyers appeared before Judge Pearson, he issued a writ of habeas corpus which directed Colonel Kirk to permit Moore to appear before the judge. Colonel Kirk refused to do this, saying that a military court was getting ready to try Moore and the other prisoners and that he could not surrender them unless Governor Holden gave him an order to do so.

The lawyers for Moore and the other prisoners then asked Judge Pearson to issue a "writ of attachment" against Colonel Kirk, which would mean that he would be arrested and brought in. They also asked the judge to send out a sheriff to bring

STATE OF NORTH CAROLINA,

To GEORGE W. KIRK, Greeting:

We Command You, That the body of Peter H. Williamson *being confined and detained in your custody, as it is said, together with the day and cause of his capture and detention, by whatever name he may be called, you have before me, RICHMOND M. PEARSON, Chief Justice of the Supreme Court of the State aforesaid, at the Chamber of the Supreme Court, in the City of Raleigh, immediately after the receipt of this writ, to do and receive what shall be then and there considered in his behalf.*

Witness. RICHMOND M. PEARSON, *Chief Justice of the Supreme Court, this the 23d day of July, A. D., 1870.*

R. M. Pearson C. J. S. C.

David A. Wicker Marshall of the Supreme Court of N.C. is hereby authorized and commanded forthwith to make service of this writ on G. W. Kirk as provided by law in such case, and make return how he has executed the same. At Raleigh July 30th 1870 —

R. M. Pearson C. J. S. C.

The original of the printed writ of habeas corpus, signed by Chief Justice Richmond M. Pearson, is with the Supreme Court file in the case of *Ex Parte Peter H. Williamson* (Appendix to Volume 64 of the *North Carolina Supreme Court Reports*, 1870).

Moore to Raleigh, even if he had to organize a posse and take Moore away from the soldiers who were guarding him. At this point the actions of both the chief justice and the governor became highly debatable. Judge Pearson decided to issue the orders Moore's lawyers had asked for, but he refused to send them out to a sheriff because he was afraid that if a civil officer tried to arrest Kirk or a posse tried to take the prisoners out of jail a civil war would break out in Alamance and Caswell counties. Judge Pearson said that the governor clearly had authority under the Shoffner Act to declare martial law in those counties, but he flatly denied that Holden had the power to deny anyone the right of habeas corpus. In line with this reasoning he issued

The handwritten writ of habeas corpus, signed by Pearson, is in the Supreme Court file in *Ex Parte Adolphus G. Moore*, 64 N.C. 802 (1870).

The original of the writ issued to the marshal of the Supreme Court commanding him to bring Adolphus G. Moore before the court is in the Supreme Court file in *Ex Parte Adolphus G. Moore*, 64 N.C. 802 (1870).

writs of habeas corpus for all the prisoners who had been arrested in the so-called Kirk-Holden War episode. But Judge Pearson did not free the prisoners, and he has been condemned ever since. In the most famous statement he ever made, he said that he had done all he could when he issued the writs, and that it was up to Governor Holden to decide what would be done with the prisoners. If the governor ordered Colonel Kirk to free the prisoners, they would go free. Otherwise they would stay in jail, be tried before a military court, and the responsibility would be on the governor.

In a long letter to Judge Pearson, Holden explained why he could not free the prisoners and turn them over to the civilian authorities. He had declared martial law in the first place because the Ku Klux Klan was in control of the two counties.

Chief Justice Richmond M. Pearson was a conscientious and controversial figure throughout the Civil War and Reconstruction periods.

Reminding the chief justice of the murders of Wyatt Outlaw and Senator Stephens, he insisted that the civil courts could not deal with the Klan because the Klan would have its members or its friends on the juries, even if anyone were brought to trial. "It would be mockery in me to declare that the civil authority was unable to protect the citizens against the insurgents [the Klansmen] and then turn the insurgents over to the civil authority," the governor wrote. The prisoners remained in jail, waiting to be tried by the military commission.

Governor Holden's refusal to honor a writ of habeas corpus issued by the state's chief justice was undoubtedly a serious mistake. He also made an error when he had Josiah Turner arrested in Orange County, which was not under military rule, and imprisoned in the Caswell County jail. The governor had no authority for such an action. He was driven to it by Turner's stinging criticisms in the *Sentinel*.

The Kirk-Holden War then took a strange and unexpected turn. One of the lawyers for the prisoners decided that the rights of the prisoners were protected by the Fourteenth Amendment, and since they were, the prisoners ought to be able to

The second page of the July 19, 1870, issue of the Raleigh *Sentinel* gives Josiah Turner's opinion of Governor Holden in nearly every item of news.

get a writ of habeas corpus from a federal court judge. Judge George W. Brooks then became the hero of the Conservatives by issuing writs for all the prisoners, including Josiah Turner. Governor Holden was shocked and disgusted. He protested to President Ulysses S. Grant, but Grant's attorney general decided that Judge Brooks had the right to free the prisoners. Holden then had no choice except to give up the fight. His enemies in the state were growing stronger, and the federal government was refusing to back him up. He ordered Colonel Kirk to take the prisoners before Judge Brooks, who set all of them free. It was a curious end to an unhappy episode. The Fourteenth Amendment had been written mainly to protect the rights of Negroes, but it was used instead to protect men who would deny Negroes their rights.

Election of 1870

While the Kirk-Holden War was arousing interest in North Carolina there was equal interest in the election of 1870. There was no election for governor that year, but everyone knew that if the Conservatives won overwhelming control of the legislature they would impeach Governor Holden and throw him out of office. Clearly it was a critical election in the political life of Holden. It was also important for the future of the Republican party. If the Republicans lost control of the legislature, it would be difficult for them to make a comeback.

The election was a disaster for both the Republican party and Governor Holden. The Conservatives won enough seats in the Senate and House of Representatives to impeach the governor. They also elected six out of the seven national representatives chosen in the election, as well as having their candidate chosen for state attorney general. It is fairly easy to explain why the Republicans were defeated so badly. Some people were angry with Governor Holden because of the way he had acted in the Kirk-Holden War; he was too much like a dictator. Others were disgusted with Republican rule in general, especially the legislature, which seemed to be run as much by Negroes and carpetbaggers as it was by scalawags. By this time the Conservatives had become more united than they had been in 1867 and 1868, while the Republicans were having some trouble agreeing with each other.

Impeachment of Holden

After the Conservatives won control of the state legislature it was only a matter of time before they impeached Governor Holden for his role in the events of the year 1870. There had been some talk of impeachment even before the election. Now most of the Conservatives demanded it. There were a few, including Zeb Vance, who thought that bringing the governor to trial would not be worth the effort and might even backfire, but the decision was made to go ahead and humiliate Holden and the Republicans by proving that the governor was guilty of criminal acts.

Impeachment is a device used by both the national and state governments to get rid of officials who have gone beyond the powers granted them by constitutions and laws. Impeachment occurs when the charge is brought; the official may be convicted or acquitted after the impeachment trial has been held. The lower house of the legislature brings charges against the executive officer and appoints managers to handle the trial. The senate is the court, and the highest judge presides over the trial. In the case of the Holden impeachment, this meant that Judge Pearson, who had played an important role in the events that brought about the trial, and who was himself threatened with impeachment, would be the presiding officer.

Just before Christmas, 1870, the House of Representatives drew up eight charges against the governor. The first two charges were that he had acted unlawfully by raising troops and sending them into Caswell and Alamance counties when there was no rebellion there and the civil authorities were in control. The next two articles concerned the arrest of Josiah Turner and John Kerr, saying that their arrest and imprisonment had been illegal. Articles five and six denounced Holden for refusing to obey writs of habeas corpus. The seventh article said that the state laws had not been followed in raising Colonel Kirk's regiment, and recited some of the actions of the troops, such as throwing Josiah Turner into a "loathsome dungeon." Finally, the House charged that it had been illegal for the governor to pay the soldiers who had served in Colonel Kirk's force. The House appointed seven men to serve as a board of managers; after the charges had been made, the managers hired three powerful Conservative lawyers —former Governor William A. Graham, former Governor Thomas Bragg, and the future United States Senator Augustus S. Merrimon. They apparently wanted to be sure that the governor did not escape conviction. Holden also had an unusually able group of five lawyers. One of them, William N. H. Smith, later became the state's chief justice, and another, Nathaniel Boyden, was an associate justice of the Supreme Court. For some reason, he asked Zeb Vance to be one of his lawyers, but Vance of course refused. It would have been strange indeed if the war governor had used his powerful influence to help Holden.

(It is of interest that Holden was converted and baptized in December, 1870, after impeachment was initiated. North Carolina newspapers took little notice of this event, but many of those of the North made colorful comments on this development.)

The trial lasted seven weeks, from February 2 to March 22, 1871. The procedure was slow; it was the first time in the history of the United States a state governor had been impeached, and 113 people testified for the governor while 57 testified against him. His lawyers either denied the truth of the charges

William A. Graham, Thomas Bragg, and Augustus S. Merrimon were employed by the board of managers of the House of Representatives to prosecute impeachment charges against W. W. Holden.

William N. H. Smith and Nathaniel Boyden were among five lawyers who defended Holden in the impeachment trial.

or admitted some of them but denied that the governor's actions had been unlawful. Actually, it probably did not make much difference what the lawyers said, since the legislature was determined to get Holden one way or another. They did acquit him on the first two charges but convicted him on all the others. Even a few of the Republicans voted against Holden on the charge that he had violated the right of habeas corpus. When the trial was over the Senate passed a resolution stating that Holden was no longer the governor and could never hold another state office. This was done by a strict party vote. After his impeachment Holden was not active in North Carolina politics. His career had been long and interesting but not very glorious. He had been a Democrat, a Whig, a Unionist, and a Republican; a secessionist and an anti-secessionist; an enemy of the Negro and a friend of the Negro. Because he changed his stand so many times the people of North Carolina never really seemed to trust him. He was able enough to become a great man, but he had failed to achieve greatness. The legislature stuck firmly by its decision never to allow him to participate in state affairs, but he held the federal office of postmaster at Raleigh for eight years.

DISAPPEARANCE OF THE KLAN

After the Kirk-Holden War, Klan activity practically stopped in the central counties of the state, but it still was a serious problem in some of the western counties, especially Cleveland and Rutherford. The Klansmen frightened the local judge so badly that he was afraid to go to court in Shelby, dragged a Republican member of the state legislature from his home and beat him, and wrecked the office of the *Rutherford Star,* one of the few remaining Republican newspapers. The leader of the Klan in that area was a newspaper editor named Randolph A. Shotwell. He apparently was not as violent and reckless as the members of his organization, but he was not able to control the activities of the Klansmen, who became worse and worse as time passed. Shotwell was the western version of Josiah Turner, using his newspaper editorials to criticize sharply the Republican party, its leaders and everything they stood for. He became the prime target of the Republicans in the political wars.

The North Carolina Republicans decided to call for the assistance of the national government in their fight against the Klan, and the response was favorable. First the United States Senate investigated conditions in western North Carolina, and denounced the Klan as a violent, unlawful, secret, Conservative

Randolph A. Shotwell wrote an autobiographical account of his life. In it he included the story of his imprisonment during the Reconstruction period.

organization. Next a joint committee of the two houses of Congress examined witnesses from all the southern states, took thirteen thick volumes of testimony, and came to the same conclusion as the committee which had investigated the situation in North Carolina. Colonel William L. Saunders, who had been the Grand Dragon of the Ku Klux Klan, became a hero of the Conservatives by refusing to answer any of the questions of the congressional investigating committee. Every time they asked him a question he would say only, "I decline to answer." It was a method of answering that has since become common in the televised investigations of the 1950's and 1960's. The committee had better luck with most of its other witnesses and came up with enough information to justify another series of laws Congress had passed allowing the federal government to intervene once more in the welfare of North Carolina and the South.

William L. Saunders is best remembered for his editing of the *Colonial Records;* his role in the Ku Klux Klan is a surprise to many people today.

The most important of the laws passed by Congress in 1870 and 1871, so far as North Carolina was concerned, was the one called the Ku Klux Klan Act. This measure resembled in several ways the anti-Klan law passed by the Republican legislature of North Carolina in 1869, the Shoffner Act, which Holden had used to justify his use of state troops against the Klan. The federal law passed in 1871 listed several acts of the kind the Klan usually committed and provided for fines and/or imprisonment of anyone caught engaging in these acts. Everyone who served on a jury in a Klan trial had to swear that he had never been a member of the Klan or any organization like it. The president was given the power to declare a certain area in rebellion and use federal marshalls or soldiers to restore law and order. The federal law went well beyond the earlier state legislation by stating flatly that the president could suspend the writ of habeas corpus. Before this particular law was passed Congress had provided for federal control of elections in the South and made it a crime to deprive any citizen of the rights guaranteed to him by the Fourteenth and Fifteenth amendments to the federal Constitution.

The national government then began its final assault on the Ku Klux Klan in North Carolina. Federal troops and United States marshalls poured into the troubled area in and around Cleveland and Rutherford counties. Hundreds of arrests followed, and at least fourteen hundred persons were indicted. Some of these were tried at the federal court in Raleigh in September, 1871, and some in the spring term, 1872. Most of those arrested were set free, but about thirty were convicted and sentenced to serve terms in the federal prison at Albany, New York. Randolph Shotwell, an editor who had repeatedly criticized the Republicans, received the heaviest sentence of all, a $5,000 fine and six years in prison. He remained in prison until he was pardoned by President Grant late in 1872.

By 1872 the reconstruction version of the Klan had disappeared. It did not reappear in North Carolina until the 1920's, then declined again until it reared its head in the troubles following the national Supreme Court's 1954 decision that schools must be desegregated. There is no question that the state was better off after the reconstruction Klan disappeared than it had been in the days of terror. The state and federal laws helped destroy the Klan, but probably the main reason for its disappearance was that it had helped the Conservative party to regain control of the state legislature. From the Klan point of view there was no longer any reason for its existence.

ELECTION OF 1872

Some historians believe that the national government was only using the presence of the Klan in North Carolina as an excuse for sending troops and marshalls into the state to help the Republicans win the election of 1872. This may be true, but there are a number of other reasons besides the election for the federal interference in North Carolina. Both parties considered the election an important one. The Conservatives hoped that they could elect their candidate for governor, Augustus Merrimon, while the Republicans were determined to hang on to at least one branch of the state government. Their candidate was Governor Tod R. Caldwell, who had served since Holden's impeachment. With the Negro vote solidly behind him, Caldwell edged out Merrimon by less than 2,000 votes out of nearly 200,000. The Conservatives again won the legislature, putting them in a position to elect the United States senator who was to be chosen that year. Merrimon had been promised the position if he was not the governor, but most of the Conservatives wanted to send Zeb Vance instead of Merrimon to Washington. When the Republicans saw that they could not get one of their own men elected they voted for Merrimon and elected him. They would do anything to defeat the war governor.

Changes in the Constitution

After 1872 much of the excitement and drama of the earlier reconstruction period had disappeared, and things began to seem more normal. The Klan was gone, federal troops were gone, the Negro was getting used to his new life of freedom. The state had not completely recovered from the war but was well on its way. Probably a great majority of the people and the politicians wanted to forget the hatred and bitterness of the war and reconstruction years. But the Conservative party leaders and their followers wanted first to undo some of the changes that had been made in their lives and in their society. They had tried stubborn resistance, even violence, and failed. Now they decided to bring about the changes they desired by altering the Constitution drawn up by the Republicans in the Constitutional Convention of 1868. They started the move to change the Constitution almost as soon as they got control of the legislature in 1870.

There were two groups of changes in the Constitution carried out at two different times and by two different methods. The first changes came in 1873, when the legislature itself passed several minor amendments and submitted them for approval by the people in a special election. At this time North Carolina adopted the practice of letting the legislature elect the trustees of the University of North Carolina and decided that the legislature should meet only every two years instead of annually. The 1873 amendments also did away with the commission which had been set up by the Convention of 1868 to codify the state law, and abolished the office of state superintendent of public works.

The constitutional changes made in 1875 were more numerous and more important than those of 1873. They were made by a convention which provided high political drama all the way from the time the convention was first proposed until the day it adjourned. The Republicans bitterly denounced the idea of calling a convention, saying that if the Constitution of 1868 were discarded Congress would pass another series of Reconstruction acts and place North Carolina under military rule again. They were afraid the Conservatives would undo much of the work they had done in 1868.

The campaign to choose delegates to the convention was extremely hard fought. The results of the election were the closest in the history of the state. Both parties had 95,000 votes and elected fifty-eight delegates to the convention. There were three independent delegates in the convention, one of whom, Dr. Edward Ransom, became president of the convention and took the side of the Conservatives. If the Republicans had gotten control for a few minutes they would have adjourned the convention permanently.

Most of the changes made in 1875 were connected directly or indirectly with the events that had occurred in the period since 1868. The provision outlawing "secret political societies" was obviously a slap at the Ku Klux Klan and similar organizations. The provisions which placed control of the county governments in Raleigh were apparently made to keep control of the counties out of the hands of either black men or white Republicans. To put it another way, the Conservatives were concentrating power at Raleigh because they knew they could use it to serve their own political purposes. They justified this important change by pointing out the fact that some of the justices of the peace elected by the people had been ignorant men. The amount which could be paid to state legislators for daily expenses and travel were fixed permanently so that no future legislators could vote themselves more money than they needed. Finally, an amendment drew a sharp color line between blacks and whites by saying that they should not go to school together or marry each other.

In view of the future history of the state, and especially in the story of the relations between white men and Negroes, 1875 was a crucial year. In speaking of the convention campaign R. D. W. Connor said: "From this campaign one may date the final decision of the Conservative party to draw the color line and take its stand regardless of consequences as a white man's party." Since the Conservatives, who could by this time be called Democrats, have controlled the state most of the time since the Reconstruction period, until recently the Negroes have been left out. And partly because they were connected with the wrong political party or not even taking part in politics at all, it was hard for them to have any influence on economic and social policies that could help or hurt them. It would have been better for the state, the Negroes, and for both parties if the black men had been welcomed by both Conservative-Democrats and Republicans. Unfortunately, around 1875 only the Republicans were willing to cooperate with the Negroes, and even they gave the impression of using the Negroes to their own advantage. At any rate, North Carolina started pushing the Negro down, at least in politics, in 1875.

TRIUMPH OF THE CONSERVATIVES

The final year of reconstruction is usually considered to be 1876. At the national level the presidential election between the Republican Rutherford B. Hayes and the Democrat Samuel J. Tilden was disputed, and Hayes found that he needed southern support. In order to win that support the Republicans made many promises, including one that they would withdraw federal troops from the South. Although they never admitted it or said so openly, the national Republican party was saying in effect that it was abandoning the Negro, giving up on the idea of creating a strong Republican organization in the South, and leaving the South to deal with the Negro and its other problems in any way that it chose.

In North Carolina, as in the nation at large, 1876 was the crucial year, the year of the "redemption," the year when Zeb Vance reappeared as the savior of North Carolinians who were stubbornly independent, proud, and opposed to outside interference in state affairs. It was the year the Conservatives, who at that time finally took the name Democrat, wrecked the Republican cause so badly that the Republicans have not yet recovered. But it was a splendid fight, one of the most dramatic and interest-rousing ones the state has ever seen. This was probably because Vance, who was always interesting and exciting to watch, was up against the ablest opponent he ever faced, Judge Thomas Settle. Settle was a man of great ability, integrity, and learning, and a good debater too. But he was no match on the stump for the honey-tongued and witty Vance, who could win an audience and hold it better than any orator North Carolina has produced. Settle was impressive in a series of joint debates between the two candidates for governor, but Vance always had the advantage because of his background as the war governor who had been put in prison only because he

Zebulon B. Vance, one of North Carolina's heroes, was born in 1830; he is pictured here as he looked at age thirty-six.

had done his duty. He was already a hero; he began to be a legend.

The election was an outstanding Democratic victory. The Democrats won the governor's race, the legislature, seven of the eight seats in Congress, and later on the election for president. In addition, all the constitutional amendments drawn up in 1875 were approved. For the Conservative-Democrats it was a time of great rejoicing. As they saw it, they had "redeemed" North Carolina, had brought all the branches of state government back into safe hands. One historian, R. D. W. Connor, summarized it by saying that "the administration of the state government passed into the hands of the party that best represented the intelligence, the property, and the patriotism of North Carolina." Freedom and equality for the Negroes would have to wait a while, and the uneducated and poor would just have to get along as well as they could on their own.

THE FARMER AFTER THE WAR

While the politicians wrangled with each other and tried to keep their parties in power, the people of North Carolina went about their day-to-day affairs, trying to make a decent life for themselves and their children. Most of them were people who in one way or another lived close to the land and depended on it for their existence. For men who lived this way the ten years after the Civil War were difficult ones. Much of their farm equipment, buildings, and fences had gone to ruin during the war. The chief villain in the destruction was not the army, but lack of love and attention. The men simply had not been at home to look after things. The land was still there of course, but before it could be fruitful a number of handicaps had to be overcome. There was a shortage of horses and mules needed for plowing and cultivation. Little money could be borrowed to buy new equipment and seed. Even when a farmer grew a good crop he would have trouble getting it to market because so many of the roads and railroads were in bad condition or destroyed. And when he did get his goods to market he found that the prices he got for them were going down. Cotton, in particular, was hard to sell for a good price. It brought only about half as much in 1875 as it did in 1865. Another burden the farmer faced was high taxes, or at least taxes higher than they should have been. The farmers were paying an unfair share of the total taxes paid to the state because of the high taxes on land at a time when prices for agricultural products were low. Because of these conditions, and some other circumstances, the value of farm land was dropping sharply during the Reconstruction period. Thousands of farmers had to sell their land because they could not pay their taxes, and when they put their farms up for sale the price of land dropped even lower.

The most important result of the hard times in agriculture following the war was the breakdown of the old plantation system and the growth of small farms. The disappearance of slavery made it extremely difficult to keep up the large plantations. If there had been plenty of money for the plantation owners to borrow they could have paid the Negroes to do the work they had formerly done, but the money was not available. This was the main reason the large farming units were broken down into smaller and smaller farms. Sometimes merchants in the towns who had been lucky enough to hang on to their money or had made a lot during the war bought the plantations and kept them going.

Men who owned land had two or three choices as to what they could do with it. They could rent it, hire men to work on it, or adopt the system called sharecropping. Neither renting the land nor hiring laborers worked very well because not many men had enough to pay rent, and not many plantation owners had enough to pay wages to their workers. So there was not really much choice in most cases. They had to use the sharecropping system. The landowner provided tools, mules, seed, and provisions for the cropper and his family. In return he received half of the crop, sometimes more and occasionally a little less.

The sharecropping system was both harmful and helpful to the farmers of North Carolina and to the state as a whole. It caused farms to get even smaller at a time when the use of machinery made it necessary to work larger farms. It caused many landowners to grow only one crop when they would have been better off growing several. But worst of all, it made it just about impossible for the croppers to overcome the condition of poverty in which most of them soon began to live. They never seemed to gain anything from their work except enough food to eat and a shack to live in.

In some ways the sharecropping system was a blessing. It at least made it possible for some people, both white and black, to earn a living which they could have earned in no other way. The state benefited from the fact that the farms kept on operating when there was little money available to keep them going.

Closely connected with the sharecropping system was what is called the crop-lien system. The farmers had to get supplies and provisions for themselves and their croppers from the merchants. Since they did not usually have enough to pay cash they gave the merchants a "lien" on the crops they had growing in the fields. They had to promise to plant cotton or tobacco or a crop that was sure to bring in money. The merchant, who was taking a big risk on the future of a crop, felt that he had to charge higher interest rates than one normally had to pay. The farmers naturally hated to be in debt to the merchants all the time, but they had little choice. The banks would not lend them the money they needed.

Within three or four years after political reconstruction ended the North Carolina farmers were producing more than they had before the Civil War. That is about the only pleasant thing that can be said about their condition. With the sharecropping, crop-lien, and "one crop" systems already fixed, and prices of what they bought higher than prices for what they sold, the farmers faced a bleak future.

GROWTH OF INDUSTRY

During the Reconstruction period there was a much more promising outlook for industry than there was for the farmers.

The war had stimulated the growth of small industries in the state because the normal sources of supply had been cut off and more goods were needed. Not all of the new war industries survived, but they had served as a training place for the men who would work and build in the postwar period. Even by 1870 the state had nearly as many manufacturing plants as it did in 1860, and the products they were turning out were much more valuable than they had been before the war. And in spite of the fact that capital was scarce, there was more money invested in industry four years after the war than there had been at the start of the conflict. At that time the leading industries were cotton, lumber, food, and building materials, but tobacco and naval stores were not far behind.

It was in the years immediately after the war that North Carolina began to build and strengthen the two industries for which it is most famous, tobacco and textiles. There has been much interest in the story of the growth of the tobacco industry, probably because it involves the colorful career of "Buck" Duke, and because it illustrates very clearly how it was possible for a poor boy to become a multimillionaire in a short time. This is exactly what Washington Duke and his sons Brodie, Buck, and Ben did. The story of their famous first sales trip in the wagon drawn by blind mules eventually reaches the ears of almost every schoolchild in North Carolina. From this humble beginning the Dukes built up the greatest tobacco business in the world. They succeeded, like other North Carolina tobaccomen, because they took advantage of an opportunity that had been partly created by the war, and because they worked hard, were willing to take risks, and sometimes formed powerful combinations to crush out the smaller and weaker tobaccomen. Durham, the site of the Duke operations, became the most important of the tobacco manufacturing towns; it had twelve tobacco factories in 1872 and was growing rapidly.

The tobacco industry grew as rapidly in Winston as it did in Durham, starting about the same time. The Winston version of the Dukes was the Reynolds family, which began its operations in 1874. By 1881 the Reynolds factory was in a brick building three stories high; it worked 125 men and turned out close to 300,000 pounds of tobacco that year. Only a few years earlier the tobacco "factories" had been log sheds on the farms where the tobacco was grown. The contrast between the log sheds and the sturdy brick factory of the Reynoldses and the booming business of the Dukes meant that North Carolina was well on its way to the leadership of the world in the production of tobacco.

The other major industry which developed rapidly during the ten years after the war was textiles. In this activity the state had a much firmer foundation to build on than it had in tobacco since the industry was firmly established before the war and boomed during the war. In the years just after the war a second generation took over the management of the prewar textile mills established by their fathers. During the 1870's several new mills were established that would provide future fortunes for their founders and benefit the whole state. The cotton mills were turning out more products in 1870 than they had in 1860, and by 1880 production had almost doubled again. Yet, impressive as this may sound, it was only after 1880 that the state made its greatest advances in the production of textiles.

THE RAILROADS

Before North Carolina could get its industrial revolution into full swing it had to have a good transportation network. The best thinkers before the war had recommended a balanced system consisting of roads, waterways, and railroads. But even before the war the state seemed more interested in building railroads than in any other kind of transport facilities. Unfortunately, during the Reconstruction period the politicians forgot all about the need for decent roads and waterways and harbors, and staked everything the state could afford on the building of railroads. The result was that the railroads were involved in the political frauds described earlier, and very little construction took place. Less than six hundred miles were built during the whole period.

There can be no doubt that the state needed a good system of rail lines. In 1865 it was impossible to travel by rail any farther west than Morganton. The line from the coast to Morganton was owned by three different companies. At the end of the war the state still dreamed of a major east-west line running all the way from Murphy to Morehead City. Such a road would channel North Carolina's products to its own coast, instead of letting them drift away to Norfolk and Charleston. The roads that survived the war were in terrible shape, although the Union army had repaired some of the lines in the territory it controlled. Some of the companies might have survived if they had been able to collect bills owed to them by the Confederate government and if they had not invested in Confederate bonds.

Regardless of these conditions and difficulties, the state did

The Licklog and McElroy tunnels are examples of construction which had to be done in order to complete the railroad through the mountains of western North Carolina.

acquire some new railroads during the Reconstruction period. The Western North Carolina Railroad, after being reorganized by the state, completed its line to Old Fort in 1869. There it encountered extreme hardships in getting over the steep mountains to Asheville and went bankrupt. The state had to buy out the company in 1875. By using convicts for labor, the railroad company soon reached Asheville and then built on toward Murphy and the Tennessee line. The Carolina Central Railway Company completed a line from Wilmington to Shelby in 1875, and in 1877 the Raleigh and Augusta Air Line finished a road it had been building from Raleigh to Hamlet.

By 1870 many North Carolinians had begun to have serious doubts as to whether the state government should be connected in any way with the building of railroads. Thirty years earlier the state had had a dream of a fine network of railroads, built by private companies, but supported generously by state money. The railroads had become involved in politics. Years had passed, but the rail system was not even near completion. The Republican legislature of 1868 and 1869 had further discredited the idea of state aid to railroads by allowing them to get bound up in corruption. There was the fact too that the government was not as well off financially in the postwar years as it had been

This map of the Mountain Division of the Western North Carolina Railroad, drawn from surveys made in 1881, clearly shows the difficult terrain on the route.

in earlier times. The result of all this was that the state began pulling out of the railroad business, turning over its interests to private enterprise. The first important step in this direction came in 1871 when the state leased the North Carolina Railroad between Greensboro and Charlotte to northern businessmen who controlled the Richmond and Danville Railroad. The businessmen forced the state to make the lease by threatening to drive the state road out of business. The final step in taking the state out of the railroad game came just after the end of the Reconstruction period when the state sold the Western North Carolina Railroad to a group from New York. This group completed the road to the Tennessee border in 1882.

RELIGION

If the Civil War created problems in the areas of politics and economics, it also left unanswered questions and unsolved problems in the field of religion. Most of the churches had divided before or during the war. Some people at least hoped that they could be reunited. But the only denomination in which reunion occurred soon after the war was the Episcopal church. Bishop Thomas Atkinson helped bring about the reunion by explaining to the general convention the southern position on some of the issues that had divided the church.

The other leading denominations refused to reunite their northern and southern branches. This was not because they differed so much about religious matters but because they could not agree on certain social questions, especially those having to do with the Negroes. The churches seem to have been affected by much of the prejudice, suspicion, bitterness, and even hatred that existed in society at large during the period. The southerners feared that northern ideas would be imposed on them. The leading Baptist newspaper in the state, the *Biblical Recorder,* was outraged when some northern churches suggested that the Negroes should be treated as equals in the churches of North Carolina. The feelings that kept the northern and southern branches of the various denominations separated were so strong that they have still not been overcome.

Suspicion of the North showed itself in other ways in the field of religion soon after the war ended. One of the biggest arguments for doing missionary and educational work in the state was that if the North Carolina churches did not do this work it would be done by missionaries from the North. These

St. Ambrose Episcopal Church, on Wilmington Street in Raleigh, was built in 1868; it was one of the churches built for a Negro congregation. The church was razed in 1965.

northern missionaries and schoolteachers might mix ideas about politics with their religious teaching, and this could undermine the way North Carolinians had thought and lived in the past. North Carolina churches did as much as they could to help establish new congregations among the freedmen, but the money they had available was so small that they did not achieve much in the first few years after the war.

One of the most important religious developments in North Carolina and the South during the Reconstruction period was the formation of Negro churches. Before and during the war the slaves had usually gone to the same services as the whites. After the slaves were freed from labor without pay they naturally wanted to be free and equal in their religious life too. But the whites who controlled the churches were not willing to allow the Negro freedom and equality in church. Whites did not want the Negroes sitting in the same pews with them or voting in church elections or sending Negro delegates to represent the black men in the higher governing bodies of the churches. As soon as the Negroes saw that they would not be treated as equals in the white churches they decided to form their own congregations and denominations. Within five years after the war Negroes from all the major denominations had formed their own churches and set up separate systems of church government from those of the whites. A few Negroes remained in the white churches, but most of them preferred to join the new churches. As a result the Negro churches grew rapidly.

THE STRUGGLE IN EDUCATION

While the churches made a rather quick revival after the war and soon passed the level of 1860, the schools and colleges of North Carolina struggled grimly just to keep themselves alive during the years of reconstruction. At the start of the war the state had had the best system of public schools in the South. It was not supported by tax money gathered each year for schools, but got most of its income from the Literary Fund, which had been set up long before the war. During the war the men in charge of the Literary Fund invested it in state and Confederate bonds and railroad stock. When the Confederacy collapsed and the state cut off income from the bonds it had issued during the war, the Literary Fund was almost wiped out. There was not enough money to support a state system of public schools, and the legislature was not willing to appropriate any from 1865 to 1868.

When the Republicans gained control of the constitutional convention and the state government in 1868 they made determined efforts to revive public education in North Carolina. The Constitution of 1868 said that "schools and the means of education shall forever be encouraged," and required the legislature to set up a system of free schools which would be open four months each year to everyone between the ages of six and twenty-one. The constitution-makers refused to state in the Constitution that Negroes had to go to schools separate from the whites. The legislature of 1868-1869 passed a school law which would have been highly successful if it had been carried out in the spirit in which it was passed. This measure authorized the commissioners of the counties to levy a school tax in each school district which would not or could not raise money in some other way. It separated white and Negro schools but declared they should be treated equally.

The law of 1869 appeared to be a promising beginning for the revival of public education, but unfortunately the results were disappointing. Several things went wrong. The most damaging thing was that in 1870, in the case of *Lane v. Stanly,* the state Supreme Court took away the powers of the county commissioners to levy enough taxes to support the four-month system required by the Constitution. The judges denied that education was a "necessary expense." They required the county commissioners to get approval of school taxes from the people of their counties in special elections, and this approval was usually impossible to get. The legislature made appropriations for the schools, but the money sometimes went to other projects. The state superintendent of schools in the crucial period after the passage of the law of 1869 was a Massachusetts carpetbagger, the Reverend S. S. Ashley, who failed to win the confidence and support of the people of the state.

By 1870 it was apparent that North Carolina's educational recovery was going to be painfully slow. At that time there were fewer children in school than there had been during the war, in spite of the fact that thousands of Negroes were then going to school. Nearly half of the people of the state over ten years old could not read and write. In 1872 the state superintendent pointed out other defects in the system in addition to those already mentioned. Many of the teachers were not fit to be in classrooms. There was no uniform system of textbooks; the laws did not provide for building and maintaining schoolhouses; and parents could not be made to send the children to school.

The reconstructed schoolhouse on the Aycock Birthplace State Historic Site is typical of those of the years following the Civil War. A modern group of students is trying the chairs and getting the feel of the nineteenth-century classroom.

One of the main functions of the Freedmen's Bureau was to teach former slaves. The photograph was furnished by the Photographic Service of the University of North Carolina Library at Chapel Hill.

These defects in the system of public education remained throughout the Reconstruction period, and for over twenty years after that. What it all amounts to is that the people of North Carolina simply did not have enough interest in education to overcome the obstacles, which undoubtedly existed. After the state's economy began to revive there was enough money for schools, and the Constitution and laws could have been rewritten in such a way as to win approval of the judges. The way to good public education existed, but there was no will to travel it.

Much of the educational work done in North Carolina during the years of reconstruction, and especially before 1870, was done by the Freedmen's Bureau and by northern religious and social organizations. In 1869 the bureau was conducting 250 schools and the private societies 150. There were about 20,000 students enrolled in these schools. Most of them were ungraded, that is, schools in which all the pupils were learning the same thing at the same time, usually just reading and writing. In some cases there would be three or four generations of the same family in a classroom. In one school a six-year-old girl started learning her alphabet at the same time as her mother, grandmother, and great-grandmother. Most of the pupils in the Freedmen's Bureau schools were Negroes who as slaves had been denied an education, but some whites also attended the schools.

The schools of North Carolina also received some help from the Peabody Education Fund, which was set up in 1867 by a wealthy northerner to help the South restore its educational system. Peabody believed in helping only those places which first demonstrated a genuine interest in education by raising money for themselves. Because of this belief, the towns which got money from the Peabody Fund were in most cases the ones which needed it the least, but the results were still good. Several better-than-average schools were established, and they served as models of what could be done when public interest in education was aroused.

The small private colleges came back to life after the war more quickly than the public school system. Trinity, Davidson, and Wake Forest had all been forced to close near the war's end by lack of students and funds, but they all managed to start their work again in 1866. Things looked grim for all of them for a few years, but by the end of the Reconstruction period they were all well on their way to complete recovery and future usefulness. The period also saw the beginning of higher educa-

Estey Hall at Shaw University was built in 1873-1874. The building was scheduled for demolition when it sustained fire damage in December, 1968. This photograph was taken from the *Biennial Report of the Superintendent of Public Instruction of North Carolina for the Scholastic Years 1896-'97 and 1897-'98.*

tion for Negroes in North Carolina when Elijah Shaw, of Massachusetts, helped establish a school at Raleigh which took the name Shaw University in 1875.

Of all the important educational institutions in the state, the University of North Carolina at Chapel Hill had perhaps the most difficult time during the postwar years. Part of the school's troubles were financial. It had heavy debts which it could not pay because the school's endowment had been wiped out through investment in Confederate bonds and stock in state banks. Almost as serious as the financial crisis was the school's deep involvement in partisan politics, which caused the people of the state to lose confidence in the university.

Up to 1868 the university had had a self-perpetuating board of trustees, one which appointed men to fill vacancies on the board as they occurred. The Constitution of 1868 said that the board of trustees of the university would consist of the State Board of Education and one member from each county; the county members were selected by the Board of Education. Under this arrangement the Republicans dominated the board of trus-

This two-room cottage designed by the famous architect Alexander Jackson Davis and built in 1858 served as the infirmary for the University of North Carolina at Chapel Hill for thirty-six years; it was, therefore, one of the buildings in use during the Reconstruction period. The photograph is from Archibald Henderson, *The Campus of the First State University*, published in 1949 by the University of North Carolina Press.

The campus of the University of North Carolina as it appeared during the presidency of David L. Swain is shown above. The photograph of the campus was furnished by the Photographic Service of the University of North Carolina Library at Chapel Hill; the inset is a picture of Swain, from the Barden Collection in the Museum of History.

tees, fired the old president of the university, David L. Swain, and replaced the faculty with relatives of the important trustees. Students stopped coming, and in 1870 the school closed.

For the next five years the Conservatives struggled to regain control of the university. They managed to change the Constitution in 1873 so that it would allow the legislature to appoint the trustees. Under this arrangement a new board of trustees, with the state's leading Conservative politician William A. Graham as its chairman, reorganized the sleeping institution at Chapel Hill and appointed Kemp P. Battle president. It would be many years before the University of North Carolina achieved greatness, but at least it had survived both poverty and politics.

Kemp P. Battle was appointed president of the University of North Carolina at a critical period in the institution's history.

Place of Reconstruction in North Carolina History

Poverty and politics. Those words almost summarize by themselves the history of North Carolina in the ten years after the Civil War, as it has been written in most of the books. There was of course much more to it than that. Not everyone was poor, and the politicians were only a small minority. There were crooked men in government, to be sure, but there were also some statesmen. While many suffered financial hardship, the state was laying the foundation for some of the outstanding industries in the world. The state began to take a new attitude toward industrial development, to believe that economic diversity rather than one crop agriculture could be its salvation. And in the realm of politics the Reconstruction period produced a vastly improved constitution which provided the basis for progress until the last half of the twentieth century.

Yet it would be false and misleading to abandon this brief study of the Reconstruction period in North Carolina on a note of optimism. The era had too much bitterness and violence and left too tragic a legacy to justify speaking of it lightly. One book about reconstruction is called *The Tragic Era*, and many North Carolinians have been moping about the "evils" of reconstruction ever since 1876. What they mean is that reconstruction was a terrible time for the state, that it shattered and weakened the state to a point from which it has not yet completely recovered. Most of this kind of thinking is sentimental and exaggerated. And it hides one of the real tragedies of reconstruction—the fact that those years left behind them an abiding race prejudice and suspicion, a degraded minority of black men, and a determined band of white men who thought they ought to be supreme. North Carolina, the South, and the nation simply abandoned the Negro, let him slip back, and possibly missed a moment of opportunity to improve his condition. That is one reason why, in the second half of the twentieth century, the nation is having to face again some of the issues of the Reconstruction period.

FOR FURTHER READING

Ashe, Samuel A'Court, *History of North Carolina* (Greensboro: Charles L. Van Noppen, Publisher, Vol. I, 1925; Raleigh: Edwards and Broughton Printing Co., Vol. II, 1925), II, chapters 60-70.

Brooks, Jerome E., *Green Leaf and Gold: Tobacco in North Carolina* (Raleigh: State Department of Archives and History, 1962).

R. D. W. Connor, *North Carolina: Rebuilding an Ancient Commonwealth, 1584-1925* (Chicago and New York: American Historical Society, Inc., 4 volumes, 1928-1929), II, chapters 36-39.

Daniels, Jonathan, *Prince of Carpetbaggers* (Philadelphia and New York: J. B. Lippincott Company, 1958).

Evans, William McKee, *Ballots and Fence Rails: Reconstruction on the Lower Cape Fear* (Chapel Hill: University of North Carolina Press, 1967).

Hamilton, J. G. de Roulhac (ed.), *The Correspondence of Jonathan Worth* (Raleigh: North Carolina Historical Commission [State Department of Archives and History], 2 volumes, 1909), II.

Hamilton, J. G. de Roulhac (ed.), *The Papers of Randolph Abbott Shotwell* (Raleigh: North Carolina Historical Commission [State Department of Archives and History], 3 volumes, 1929-1936), II and III.

Hamilton, J. G. de Roulhac *Reconstruction in North Carolina* (New York: Columbia University, Longmans, Green & Co., agents [Vol. LVIII of *Studies in History, Economics and Public Law,* edited by the Faculty of Political Science of Columbia University], 1914).

Heyman, Max L., "The Great Reconstructor: General E. R. S. Canby and the Second Military District," *North Carolina Historical Review,* XXXII (January, 1955), 52-80.

Holden, William W., *Memoirs of W. W. Holden* (Durham: Seeman Printery, 1911).

Lefler, Hugh Talmage, and Albert Ray Newsome, *North Carolina: The History of a Southern State* (Chapel Hill: University of North Carolina Press, c. 1954), chapters 33-37.

Lefler, Hugh Talmage (ed.), *North Carolina History Told by Contemporaries* (Chapel Hill: University of North Carolina Press, third edition, c. 1956), chapters 10 and 11.

Morrill, James Roy III, "North Carolina and the Administration of Brevet Major General Sickles," *North Carolina Historical Review,* XLII (Summer, 1965), 291-305.

Olsen, Otto H., *Carpetbagger's Crusade: The Life of Albion Winegar Tourgée* (Baltimore: Johns Hopkins Press, 1965).

Olsen, Otto H., "The Ku Klux Klan: A Study in Reconstruction Politics and Propaganda," *North Carolina Historical Review,* XXXIX (Summer, 1962), 340-362.

Tourgée, Albion Winegar, *A Fool's Errand: By One of the Fools* (New York: Fords, Howard, and Hulbert, 1880).

Zuber, Richard L., *Jonathan Worth: A Biography of a Southern Unionist* (Chapel Hill: University of North Carolina Press, 1965).